CONVICTION

HOW I OVERCAME MY TRAUMATIC PAST AND FOUND MY PURPOSE

NORLIZA PAVLAKOS

Conviction © 2025 Norliza Pavlakos

All Rights Reserved. No part of this book may be reproduced in any form or by any electronic or mechanical means including information storage and retrieval systems, without permission in writing from the author. The only exception is by a reviewer, who may quote short excerpts in a review.

This book is a work of non-fiction. This publication is designed to provide accurate and authoritative information in regards to the subject matter covered. It is sold with the understanding that neither the author nor the publisher is engaged in rendering legal, investment, accounting, or other professional services. These are the memories of the author, from their perspective, and they have tried to represent events as faithfully as possible.

Printed in Australia

Cover and internal design by Book Burrow

www.bookburrow.com.au

First printing: January 2025

Paperback ISBN 978-1-7637621-0-7

eBook ISBN 978-1-7637621-1-4

Hardback ISBN 978-1-7637621-2-1

www.norliza.com

Distributed by Lightning Source Global and IngramSpark

A catalogue record for this work is available from the National Library of Australia

DISCLAIMER

Conviction is a deeply personal account of my life, shared with honesty and raw emotion. It addresses sensitive and potentially distressing themes, including physical and emotional violence, abduction, suicide, and assault. Please consider this before deciding to read. If you or someone you know needs support, I encourage you to visit mymindhub.com.

ACKNOWLEDGMENTS

To my mother, Patma Ghani — Mummy, thank you for being my greatest teacher. To my godmother, Hanis Hussein — Your love has shaped me into who I am today. To my Aunt Mumtaz Begum — Thank you for showing me the true meaning of dignity. To Nick Pavlakos — Thank you for believing in me, pushing me forward, and being a loving father to our children. To my brothers, Sharul and Deen Ariff — Our bond is unbreakable. To Jocelyn Hew — You've been my rock in the darkest times. I am forever grateful. To Jennifer Henriksen — Thank you for reminding me of the quiet strength found in faith. To Samuel Dowle — Your love has inspired me to believe in love, with each letter deepening my strength.

To Jihan Martin, Snezana Mitrovic, Nicole Forsyth Burton, Natalie Shand, Rue Desilva, Selin Samiloglu, Celine Cenik, Zuzana Lojovah, Ijeoma Nduneri, Ujunwa Ogbonna, Rosie Quinn, Nausheen Abdul Aziz, Ricky Singh, Adrian and Michelle Lyssenkoff, Marie Pangaud, Matt and Raquel Iuliano, Peter Rosetzky, Stefan Zabielski, Claire Halliday, Veena Parwardhan, Sarah Chrome, Andrea Costa, Alyson Pendlebury, and Alana Lambert — Some of you have supported me personally, others professionally. Thank you for being part of my journey. To everyone who has read my story, listened to my audiobook, or attended my talks — May my words inspire you, just as your support has inspired me.

DEDICATION

To my beautiful children — Adam, Alexii, Alyana, Azahra, and Amira — being your mummy is my ultimate blessing. I hope this book will stand as a legacy of your self-belief and a testament to your potential. I believe in you. When I am no longer in this world, let this book be a reminder of Mummy's love for all of you.

CONTENTS

PART ONE: **Introduction**

3	Recognise Your Own Value...
7	Crisis Management
23	Loss
38	Drowning in Despair
48	Running Away
53	Toxic Love
58	Secrets and Lies
65	Ambitions and Awareness
71	Hitting Rock Bottom
78	Turning the Corner

PART TWO: **Regaining Control**

89	A New Beginning
103	Loving Again
116	Closing an Ugly Chapter
125	The Power of Reflection
130	Trouble in Paradise
139	Hanover House
146	Rediscovering Love and Recognising Signs
157	A New Chapter
161	Making Peace With My Parents
178	People, Passion and Putting My Life at Risk
191	My Mind Hub: Empowering Minds
196	Purpose, Trust, Success and Discovery: Healing from the Ravages of PTSD
199	The Signs are There Don't Forget to Look
204	Dare To Be Extraordinary
206	Things Take Time, and Time Can Change Things

208	It's Okay to Admit You're Imperfect
209	Choose to Change Your Narrative

PART THREE: Conviction in Action: Tools for Change

215	Inner Strength
217	Build Your Inner Strength
220	Acceptance
223	Open Your Mind to Acceptance
225	Learn to Forgive
226	Self-forgiveness
229	Self-determination
231	Living with Self-determination
232	Magical Thinking
236	Resourcefulness
238	Reward Yourself for Resourcefulness
239	Practical Thinking
241	Make Practical Thinking a Daily Habit
242	Resilience
246	Responsibility
249	A Winning Mindset
252	The Courage of Conviction
255	Focus
257	Practical Ways to Sharpen Your Focus
259	Perseverance
263	Self-esteem
266	Commitment
269	True Happiness
272	Excellence
275	Utilise Neuroplasticity
276	Self-confidence
278	Inner Peace
281	A Purpose in Life

PART ONE

INTRODUCTION

RECOGNISE YOUR OWN VALUE...

Don't plead for warmth from others.
Ignite it from the fire within.

I was still a couple of years away from finding my motivational speaking feet when the inspiration for this book sparked a new light inside me. In my personal life, I'd risen above some soul-destroying adversities. Professionally, I'd built all the typical hallmarks of a 'successful' life as a businesswoman with a powerful income.

I was keen to write something for the benefit of other victims of trauma and abuse and explain how - despite circumstances that stretched back to childhood and created an unstable foundation of doubt, mistrust, fear and self-loathing - I was able to overcome my past and find my purpose. I imagined creating a book that would reveal how I turned my shambolic life around and evolved from zero self-esteem and zero self-confidence, to unwavering self-belief in my knowledge that I am capable of tackling whatever life throws at me.

My story didn't always have the prospect of a happy ending. Once upon what seems like a long, long time ago, I was a disempowered, voiceless victim of childhood sexual abuse, rape, abduction, a violent marriage and the self-medicating drug addiction that was my attempt to dull my emotional, psychological and often, physical pain.

Today, as a motivational speaker, I draw on these personal experiences to prove that, when it comes to achieving goals, there is nothing that can stop you. I believe that success is possible, not because of unrealistic hope, but because of my commitment to seek the healing knowledge that helps me access powerful levels of determination and ambitious self-belief.

Creating strength from what had once been pain and humiliation, has not been easy. Believe me, though, when I tell you that it is possible. Writing this book has not been easy either. The objective behind sharing such intimate details of my life was not to hurt anyone and certainly not to cause embarrassment or discomfort for my loved ones.

By telling my own story of grit and resilience, I hope to shine a light on the idea that tapping into your own resilient spirit is achievable, even after spending a lifetime believing that spirit is crushed. This book is not written as a trauma-fest, where I share each difficult description of the many things that have happened across numerous years of my life in graphic detail. By choice, I have omitted many of the finer details of the trauma I have lived through, because that's not what this book needs to spell out. If you have experienced similar pain, I am sure you will appreciate that and understand. The lessons I want to share are bigger than explaining how many times I have been hurt or let down by someone I trusted.

My journey through a highly abusive, destructive, personal storm goes beyond survival to unlock the potential of empowerment and hope. I don't claim to have all the answers but the life skills I share in part three of the book, for regaining control in my own life, I believe they have the power to help you too.

Whether you're a small business owner, a team member,

someone carrying the responsibility of a senior management position or immersing yourself in the life of a stay-at-home parent, all the skills I share have the potential to take you a step closer to a more rewarding outcome. When you break the negative thought patterns that wreak havoc in your mind, you can uncover the encouragement and motivation to access your own inner strength, find your voice and become the person you were meant to be, no matter how big the obstacles in your way might seem. The fact that I am still here to write this to you is irrefutable proof that, when fuelled by the right thoughts, our mind can truly be an enabling agent of change.

When selfish people cross our paths, those encounters can change the direction of our lives so horribly that the goals we were once so committed to seem beyond our grasp. Instead, we can feel as though we are teetering on the precipice of a deep, dark mine of despair. It only takes a small shove from another to push us in.

Once we start our descent, it's often hard to stop falling and, because the ability to climb out can feel so beyond reach, we sometimes choose to stay at the bottom. Worse still, we even end up believing that we belong there and so sabotage the opportunities that present ways for us to rise. Some of the selfish people I encountered in my life were those I loved and trusted. How can an uncle say he loves his young niece, yet touch her in ways he knows is wrong? Why does family pride and reputation come before the wellbeing of a child? These incidents were the starter gun for a relay of events that threw me into that dark mine and kept me buried there for a very long time.

It took me a while to understand that, for me, sustainable healing was about accepting what had happened in my life and finding a way to move on. But the most significant part of my healing was realising that, even when I felt as if I was in the deepest, blackest pit of hopelessness, the prospect of mining the diamonds within my most painful experiences helped me keep going. I couldn't change what happened in my past, but I could take control of my future by making the choice to find the sparkling gems of learning I'd achieved amidst the chaos and steer my life in the direction that I wanted it to head.

That direction was upwards but climbing out of the mine wasn't enough. I sifted through all the heartache and pain deep inside me and took the diamonds with me. I could hold on tightly to the bright, shiny, valuable parts of me, wherever and whatever got in my way. I hope that my story will remind you that there are precious moments of knowledge, self-discovery and resilience within your own experience too. Hold on to them.

Trauma can be devastating and, depending on the cause, it can be so severe that overcoming it and regaining emotional balance may be virtually impossible without the added support structure of professional help and tailored therapy. If you're currently working with a trauma specialist or believe you need to reach out to one, the story outlined in this book could inspire you to feel understood.

Just remember: the stronger your desire to heal and succeed, the more committed you'll be to retraining your mind and pursuing your goals. My wish for you is that, by the time you get to the last page of this book, you will want to take action to discover the untapped power within you. It's there. Trust me.

When you realise you are capable of achieving so much more, making the important commitment to never give up on your dreams is a positive step toward a better way to enjoy a more rewarding life. You've waited long enough.

CRISIS MANAGEMENT

1997, Melbourne

It was one of those gently fragrant evenings, full of possibility. Soft, warm air and a wide-open sky was already transforming from pale blue to pretty lavender as the sun dipped a little lower towards the horizon. I was feeling good about myself. It was a feeling I hadn't experienced in a while.

It felt like freedom.

Another day of uni was over and I was racing to get ready, before the short walk to meet friends at a favourite South Yarra café, Chapelli's. I'd chosen my best outfit and I smoothed my palms gently over the navy skirt and matching top before leaning closer towards the bathroom mirror and reaching for my eyeliner. By the time I reached Oxford Street, my mind was buzzing with thoughts about my future. I still couldn't imagine exactly what it might look like, but after the upheaval of trading life in my unhappy family home with the stress of living on Centrelink benefits as a 16-year-old, alone in apartment accommodation as I tried my hardest to complete my secondary education, then the even lonelier realisation that my idea of the perfect boyfriend turned out to be a controlling, violent abuser, I was officially single again. And loving it.

I was almost at Chapel Street when I noticed a well-built man leaning against a flashy car. As I strode past him, he stopped me and asked me my name.

'I'm a talent scout,' he said, 'and you're going to be the next Nike model!'

I stared back, still thinking of what my reaction should be to his pitch. He continued.

'You're exactly the kind of girl we're looking for. I can't wait to tell the heads of Channel 10 about you at tonight's meeting.'

He held up a folder with Channel 10 inscribed on it and then waved an identification card at me. I'd passed the television channel's office building in my suburb many times, so it didn't seem ridiculous that he really could be an employee there. But despite seeing the well-known TV channel's letterhead poking from the folder and the way he flashed what looked like a Channel 10 business card, I still felt this was too good to be true.

My silence held me there as his smooth delivery continued, about how I could probably earn $10,000 from the ad campaign, after they flew me to Hawaii for the shoot. The bleat of his mobile phone cut through his story and, when he answered it, he told the person on the other end, 'I have her – the perfect model. The face, everything. I'll bring her in.'

The interruption snapped me back into the moment and my original mission to meet my friends. I told him I had to go and reached for his contact details.

'I'll take your business card and speak to my parents. I need their permission for this,' I said.

The tone of his reply was friendly, but still somehow urgent.

'Sure, do that. But you'll have to hurry and let me know, the sooner the better. I think you would be perfect for the job.'

He walked around his car and got into it quickly, as if he'd remembered he had to be somewhere in a hurry. I watched as he leaned across the car to open its glovebox. He pulled out a notepad, leaned over a bit more and opened the passenger door.

'Here.' He stretched across further to hold the notepad toward me. 'Write your name and number and I'll call you.' He pointed to the passenger seat. 'Don't worry. Sit and write down your details for me.'

The light was not yet fading. From where I stood, I could see Chapelli's and my friends already at one of the outdoor tables. Shazia was there, with two others from our group next to her. My friend was tall and gorgeous and already establishing her reputation in the modelling world. In that instant, I thought of the way Shazia grabbed opportunities that came her way. I wanted to be like her. Opportunities were things I often wished would land in my direction and now, right here, on the familiar streets of my own neighbourhood, one was beckoning me.

I sat on the edge of the passenger seat with one leg inside the car and the other leg still outside, with the sole of my shoe steady against the footpath. I wrote my name in his notepad. Next, my number.

There was a knot tightening in my stomach. I didn't recognise it was my instinct warning me to get out. With my starry eyes and my inexperience, I misinterpreted the jolt inside me as something different. Part nerves, part excitement and the hint of potential.

The car started suddenly and the man swung the steering wheel into a tight, fast u-turn that slid me deeper into the car seat as the passenger door slammed shut. The sound of the door locks trapping me there rang through my head, followed by the horrified realisation that something terrible was happening. All I could think of now was how I could escape from the dangerous situation I'd stupidly got myself into.

'Where are you taking me? Please, please let me go.'

I was gasping at the words, wishing desperately that I could somehow turn the clock back and be safe again. The man didn't speak and simply kept driving.

The strange silence made me grasp the awful truth. I'd been abducted. I thought back to the classroom "stranger danger" warnings that came with cheaply shot videos of creepy looking men trying to tempt little children with promises of lollies. Here I was, almost a woman and lured with the sweet promise of a modelling career and the chance at the financial independence I'd been craving for so long.

No matter how many times I begged him to let me go, he ignored me and kept driving – the thrum of the engine whining and rumbling as we slowed and sped up again through several intersections. The tinted windows were closed, and I had no idea where we were heading or what was going to happen next. Now, he was yelling at me.

'You're a bitch! You're fucked and you're going to die!'

He started relating details about my personal life and my fear rose. He knew who I was! He'd targeted me and, like a fool, I fell into his trap. Then the man let the windows down, just a little. I saw my chance and screamed with all the lung power I had.

'Help! Help me, please. I've been kidnapped!'

I expected immediate action from anyone who might have heard my panicked voice but, instead, people simply walked past, indifferent to my desperate appeals.

'See? Even they know that you're shit, that you're a runaway no one cares about.'

The windows closed again and, as he looked at me, an ugly grin split his face. He kept driving. I wrestled against the door handle and banged the window glass with my fist, but nothing budged. His hand grabbed at my arm and squeezed it so hard that a squeal of pain pushed out of me, like air rushing from a punctured tyre.

I quickly realised no amount of struggling could free me from this situation. Forcing myself to stay calm and still and trying to not give in to the feeling of disorientation that was washing over me, became my focus. I vaguely noticed we were slowing down. When we finally stopped, we seemed to be in a secluded park with dense foliage that blocked the view from the street.

At the time, I'd thought we were far away from South Yarra; the bush and the darkness as evening set in had deceived me. I had no idea where I was or what he was about to do to me. The horrifying wonder of it all felt like a sharp, heavy weight in my lungs, making it harder for them to move inside me. Harder to let my breath in and out.

My kidnapper parked the car and screamed at me.

'You're a bitch and a slut. Take off your top.'

A shiver of fear made me visibly twitch. I did what he told me.

'No! Not that,' he yelled. 'Take off your skirt.'

I pulled my top back down with fumbling hands and took off my skirt. He threw another dirty look at me.

'Your top, you bitch. Take it off!'

I felt like I was his puppet and I moved through the motions of every order he barked at me, as if the control of my limbs and my fate was entirely in his hands. When he started to molest me, my tears only seemed to encourage him.

It went on for what felt like hours. He seemed to love the control he had over me and his torture of my tender skin alternated between pinching, choking and sexually assaulting me. He told me to put my top and underwear back on and snapped at me to get out of his car. In the dark of the park, he gestured toward two trees that were ahead of us and gave me another instruction.

'Walk from that tree to that one. Go on!'

I stumbled from the car, trembling and terrified of what was going to happen next. Thoughts of making a dash for it raced through my mind but I remembered my ID and wallet still in my bag inside his car and I imagined him coming for me again. Tracking me down. I didn't know where I was, anyway. Where could I possibly run to? The bushes all around us and the lack of people walking or driving past throughout the whole attack gave the impression that we were in a deserted area, perhaps kilometres away from help of any kind. I could keep screaming until my voice gave out, but who would hear me?

The fear made me breathless as I staggered across the distance between the two trees. He ordered me back to the car and I obeyed and then immediately regretted it, wondering what might have happened if I'd simply run in the opposite direction instead. The clothing he'd just demanded me to put on again, now had to come off. He was screaming it at me.

I felt his filthy hands all over my body again and the verbal abuse continued. When the sharp pain of his fingers rammed into me, I tried hard to shut out the stinging heat of his rough groping, but the shock of it only seemed to make the pain more intense.

I saw the glint of a large, sharp blade as he waved a hunting knife.

'Okay. Time for me to put you out of your misery.'

He was going to murder me and dump my body in the Yarra River. I was sure of it. He pushed the passenger seat back and slowly, almost gently, ran the knife over my naked body, around my breasts and along my belly and then back up and around my breasts again. The way he went from screaming at me and hurting me, to these gentle, controlled motions sent a shiver through me. My pulse quickened, muscles tensing with the fear of what might come next. Was he savouring my terror before killing me or was he contemplating sparing my life?

The knife pressed into my skin. I couldn't bear the thought of him cutting my breasts off. That would surely be much scarier and more painful than if he just thrust the knife into me and got it over with. His sudden shout startled me.

'You've got ten seconds to live. Say your last words before I kill you!'

Do any of us really know how we would react in a crisis? Until we're in it? What flooded through me next was a sense of quiet calm. I couldn't believe this was how I was going to die - at the hands of an angry stranger. Yet, it was as if I'd accepted it. Who would miss me if I died? I had no husband or children. The only person I could think of who would genuinely mourn me dearly was my mum. I pictured her for a moment, then let the image go.

A deep sense of peace stilled me. Fragments of seconds felt like minutes. If this lunatic wanted to see me die screaming, I wasn't going to give him that thrill. He would have to murder a quiet victim. Until that moment, I couldn't have imagined I was one of those people who could look death in the eye and not flinch. But not flinching is exactly what I did.

It wasn't bravery. I'd never been more afraid in my life. All my life, I'd been brought up to believe that God was watching over me and what happens after death is a special kind of peace. It had to be better than this. I looked at the night sky through the car windscreen and then turned to face him.

'You're going to hell,' I whispered. I felt ready. But nothing happened.

My kidnapper stared at me, speechless, his knife still pressed against my skin. Without understanding it at the time, by not screaming, begging or fighting for my life, I'd taken his power away.

It was education in its purest, most practical form. I saw a chink in his tactics. Maybe I could survive this, after all. Could I negotiate with him? Could I convince him to release me?

I didn't feel that I was capable of this kind of courage, yet now courage was strengthening my resolve. I wanted to live.

'You're not going to kill me.' The words left my lips matter-of-factly. 'How are you going to fuck a dead woman? Remember I got into your car willingly? I really want to have sex with you, you know. But the thing is, my husband is waiting at home for me. If I don't come home, he'll call the police. And, well, I don't want you to get in trouble.'

I began telling him all the things we could do in bed and how I'd love to meet up with him regularly. All I hoped for was, it would be enough to stop him from killing me then and there, that it would be enough to make him let me go. I felt the pressure of the knife relax. The man's eyes seemed to shine in the dark, like a tiger.

'Okay, I'll tell you where to meet me. You don't show up and I'll come and find you.'

He suggested the quieter end of Chapel Street and told me I needed to meet him there soon. He would drop me home first. I dressed and sat nervously in the passenger seat, trying to figure out my next move. We were getting closer to my place when I pointed at buildings on a nearby street.

'There. That's where I live.'

The idea he'd been stalking me for some time and might have known my actual address made me doubt my decision, but as he pulled the car towards the kerb, he didn't show any signs that he thought anything was strange.

'You better do as you've promised, or I'll be back.'

I got out of the car and waited for a few seconds as he drove off, then ran faster than I'd ever run in my life. I could feel the pain in my chest and legs as I sprinted, but I kept moving. It must have been more than two kilometres to my apartment, but my feet couldn't stop until I was up the stairs that led me safely inside, behind the locked door. Home.

In the shower, I fell to the floor, sobbing. It felt like a miracle I was free again. It wasn't my day to die. As the hot water fell onto my skin, against the pain he'd left there, I became aware of my phone ringing in the other room. It stopped after a while, then rang again as I stepped from the shower. I hesitated a moment, then reached for it.

Natalie, a good friend from my high school days, wanted to go out. The moment I heard her voice, I burst into tears. I blurted out what had happened and my fear that if I didn't meet him as I'd promised, he would come for me again. Natalie told me to stay calm. She was going to call the police, then come over straight away. I wouldn't be alone. Around 20 minutes later, there was a loud knock on my door. A male voice called to me.

'Open up. It's the police.'

My shaking seemed uncontrollable. Had that man come for me like he said he would? I peered through the peephole and saw four uniformed police officers outside my door. I let them in and spent several minutes explaining the details of what had happened. As they continued with their questions, more police arrived. My small apartment was now filled with about 10 male and female sergeants. They were on a mission to catch this man and they needed me to be a part of their sting operation.

'No, I can't do it!'

The horror of what I'd been through was too raw. Logically, I knew I was safe with them but the fear of putting myself anywhere near that disgusting man was too real and new.

One of the male officers sat on the couch beside me. His voice was gentle but firm.

'Liza, if you don't agree to do it, we won't be able to catch him.'

I shook my head. I didn't want to see him again. I couldn't possibly even look at him.

'You'll be fine.' The officer was doing his best to reassure me. 'We'll all be there with you. You won't be alone.'

'But what if he stabs me or shoots me?' My fear felt like a vice around my chest.

'You'll be wearing a bulletproof vest,' the policeman said. 'We'll have unmarked police cars in the street. You won't be alone, I promise you.'

He finally convinced me that it was better to catch him now, than risk him coming back later for me.

'Okay,' I said, 'but I want my friend Natalie to come along too.'

Natalie hugged me and nodded.

'I'm with you in this, Liza. Don't be afraid.'

The police waited as I prepared myself for the meeting. They pointed to where the plain-clothes police officers and unmarked police cars would be. Even as I listened to them, my coping-with-stressful-situations mechanism kicked in. I imagined we were acting out a movie scene. It wasn't really me in the scene. I was just an observer.

The bulletproof vest felt snug against me, but I worried it was noticeable, even in the dark. I was left standing at the meeting place where my kidnapper was supposed to join me. The knowledge that two policemen were hidden behind pillars close by gave me some sense of comfort. Natalie was near too, in one of the unmarked cars.

When the man finally pulled up in his car and ordered me to get in, the trembling took over and froze me to the spot. From behind the pillar near me, I could hear one of the policemen whispering to me, 'Just stay where you are.'

When I didn't get in the car, as the man had told me, he climbed from the driver's side, and yelled again.

'Get inside the fuckin' car! You stupid, black bitch.'

Then he got back into his car and drove off. Immediately, multiple sirens went off. The police cars, including the one Natalie was in, took off after him. Minutes later, the police who were with me, told me he'd been cornered somewhere on the south-eastern freeway.

My tears wouldn't stop. As the police walked me back to my apartment, they told me they had the kidnapper's car and found the evidence they needed: the knife I'd described and a gun, as well. I couldn't believe how close I'd come to dying.

Natalie spent the night with me. The next morning, I rang Mummy and Daddy. I had never envisaged making a phone call to my parents to tell them I'd been abducted and almost murdered but, if I had, I know it shouldn't have played out like it did.

In my bedtime story-esque version of me telling my parents about the trauma I'd just been through, they would have comforted me, asked if I was okay and rushed straight over to be by my side and nourish me with some comfort food and warm, tender hugs. But that's not what happened.

My parents didn't want any details. They just refused to listen. A few days later, when I saw a report about it in the newspaper, I pointed it out to my mother, but she waved me away and told me she didn't want to read or talk about it.

I'd just escaped from the clutches of a predatory kidnapper, but for my parents, it was as if I hadn't been abducted at all. Had the whole thing happened inside my head? Or was the attack against me something so trivial, so inconsequential, that no one wanted to know about it? The apathy of my parents was more than I could bear.

The police put me in contact with CASA (Centre Against Sexual Assault). But this wasn't only a sexual assault; this was an abduction. No matter who I spoke to, no one seemed to really understand the extent of what I'd been through.

The therapist's questioning seemed to focus on asking me what I'd worn that day. I don't think her intention was to denigrate me, but the state I was in, vulnerable and helpless, I couldn't process what was going on. It felt like I took everything the wrong way, but it also felt like everyone was telling me that it was somehow my fault.

I pinned all my hopes on the one final avenue I felt sure could help me heal - the judicial system. I knew it wouldn't happen quickly, but I convinced myself that seeing that man punished by the courts would help me deal with the whole horrific incident and somehow put the trauma behind me.

As I waited for those legal wheels to turn though, the lonely nights in my apartment seemed long and, even though it wasn't rational, the police had caught him after all, I was filled with a stress that my attacker was going to storm in one night and pick up where his awful assaults had left off.

On the day of the hearing, my best friend, Jocelyn, came with me to the courthouse. The fact that I was seated close to the police made me feel safe. But then a couple of police officers started to whisper to each other.

'He has a QC.'

My lack of knowledge was genuine.

'What's a QC?'

An officer explained it meant Queen's Counsel and these people were experts in the field of legal defence. I tried to remain positive, but my uncertainty of the entire process was palpable. If even the police seemed worried about their ability to prove a case against a QC, what would that mean for me?

When it was my turn to take the stand, I swore on the Holy Quran, ready for the truth to be told and justice served. The QC started questioning me about things I thought were irrelevant.

'Did you run away from home when you were 16?'

'Yes,' I said.

'Have you attempted suicide several times?'

'Yes,' I said again.

His interrogation style shocked me. After all, I hadn't tried to commit suicide in the kidnapper's car. What actually happened was, I was on my way to have a fun night with friends and someone had tried to kill me.

Then, I was asked if I'd been in an abusive relationship with a man named Gaz for the last two years. I hesitated, unsure what my toxic relationship with a good-looking, ambitious man I once believed I might marry, until his violence against me became too painful to ignore, had to do with these legal proceedings against a stranger who'd kidnapped and abused me.

To add to the complexity of my confusion, this court case was bringing that toxic relationship back into focus in many ways and not just because of the QC's investigation into my previous relationship with an abusive man. Even though my relationship with Gaz had finally ended after too many months of him using me as his punching bag, the stress of this abduction case had led me back into his violent arms for support and comfort. Something that horrified my friends.

Was I branded with some invisible sign that guided

perpetrators in my direction? Trauma specialists say that perpetrators tend to wear their victims down. They achieve this with abuse that may be masked as passionate, temporary loss of self-control or with ongoing harassment that is rebranded as a form of protective supervision.

Victims, who typically find themselves in the situation they are in because of an already-damaged sense of self-worth, tend to feel deeper levels of shame and self-blame. These relentless feelings of unworthiness and disempowerment often intertwine with an almost narcissistic sense of an ability to tap into secret powers.

I can be the one to change this. If I am patient enough, quiet enough, good enough, pretty enough, I will make this better. I will fix him.

Throughout that toxic relationship with Gaz, my friend, Jocelyn, saw things differently. She was convinced the boyfriend, whose sculptured features and slicked back hair had once made me breathless, would end my life. But by the time that life I had chosen to share with Gaz had become a knife-edge, tip-toe to survive, each increasingly violent and diminishing assault on my broken body and my damaged soul, his sweetly spoken apologies and manipulations only ever felt like love to me.

I snapped back into the courtroom, into the orbit of yet another abuser. This time, though, there was no confusion in my mind about my feelings toward him. I opened my mouth to ask why they were asking about my past instead of what had just happened at the hands of a stranger, when the QC barked, 'Yes or no?'

'Yes,' I stuttered.

I looked at the police prosecutor for help, but he turned his eyes from me to the pad in front of him and started scribbling notes on it. The QC asked another question.

'Are you struggling financially?'

Before I could answer, he continued, painting a picture of how attractive his wealthy client would look to someone like me. I still hadn't realised what the QC was up to as I left the stand and took my seat near the police prosecutor. Without any actual witnesses to the incident, it seemed like the whole case had come down to the defendant's word against mine.

The QC called their last witness. I expected it to be someone who would say how "nice" the defendant was, or what a "respectable person" he was. A pleasant looking Italian man in his forties took the stand. By this time, I was tired and wanted to go home. I didn't pay too much attention to what he was saying until I heard him say, '…the defendant's girlfriend' and 'I've seen them arguing regularly in our street for the last six months.'

Our street?

I stared at him in shock. He was calling me the defendant's girlfriend! Who was this man? I'd never ever seen him before and I hadn't seen the defendant before the day he'd kidnapped me, either. But the court seemed ready to believe their version of things. I couldn't believe what was happening.

I turned and looked at my abductor. He looked at me as casually as if he'd just paid me for his petrol at the service station, then looked away again. I jumped to my feet and yelled, 'That's a lie. It's not true!'

The judge was stern.

'Contain yourself or you will be removed from the courtroom.'

The entire proceedings seemed to end too quickly. The judge decided there would be no trial for kidnapping, deprivation of liberty or even sexual assault. All the charges against the defendant were dismissed, except for the gun being in the car at the time of the incident. A violent perpetrator who had plucked me, against my will, from an inner-city street and terrorised me, left the courtroom with a smug look on his face and a $100 fine.

When I walked outside the building, I stumbled into a horde of media and cameras flashing in my face. The reporters were looking for a sound grab and prodded me about a message for other victims.

'I was abducted and almost murdered and yet this man got away with lying. I want to tell all the victims of rape, abuse and abduction, not to be disheartened, even if the judge in the court says their trauma never happened.'

How could they tell me what did and didn't happen when I'd lived through the attack and they'd simply shuffled some papers in the court and made their minds up? I'd always believed if my parents couldn't protect me, the law would. Instead, the judge had sided with my assailant. I felt sick, thinking about each missed opportunity that could have prevented what happened to me – the people who ignored my screams for help from the car and the man in court who declared I was the kidnapper's lover.

Despite being brought up in a family that embraced spirituality, where faith felt like the secure stitching that held our values and lifestyle together, my relationship with my beliefs changed after the kidnapping. If I had been abandoned by the faith, I believed would always protect me, and all I was left with was people who wanted to take advantage of me, what future was waiting for me? The lack of emotional support from my parents made it harder for me to cope.

Taking life one day at a time was something that made it easier to rise from my bed each morning and see what the day might deliver. But the past still had its hold on me and my self-pitying introspection, questioning why things like this seemed to consistently happen to me, was something I knew I had to deal with better, to keep surviving.

LOSS

The beginning
1976-1990, Malaysia

To the west of Kuala Lumpur, Malaysia's glittering capital city, nestles one of the country's wettest cities, Petaling Jaya. The place where I was born.

My mother was a celebrity pastry chef with her own cookery show on Malaysian TV and my father was a successful radiographer at a local hospital. We, my parents, older brother Sharul and me, lived in a large, two-storey, semi-detached house with maids who attended to all the domestic work. I even had a personal maid to help care for me when Mummy and Daddy were away from home on work; something that happened too frequently for my liking.

Despite their business, my parents tried their best to make time for Sharul and me. I particularly loved spending Sunday afternoons with them at the Commonwealth Club in nearby Kuala Lumpur. Daddy would pretend to be a shark in the swimming pool and let me cling to his back as he swam to the deep end. After the four of us worked up an appetite, my parents would order hot chips, Coke, ice-cream and sweets for us to gorge on. Then Mummy would take over to keep me entertained, jumping back into the water as if she was a dolphin and returning to the pool's edge so I could feed her chips. Sharul and I were always the focus of our parents' attention the entire time we were at the club. And we loved it.

My early childhood was carefree, happy, and as normal as that of any other privileged kid in that time and place. Until, at around the age of six, a trusted favourite uncle from my father's side of the family changed everything. He told me he was only showing his love for me. By the time I was eight, as his behaviour with me escalated, my fear of him grew.

Uncle lived in a town around a three-hour drive away. But, with both my parents being working professionals, Mummy busy with her cooking demonstrations and frequently having out-of-town video shoots, they often trusted him to visit and look after us in their absence. I longed to tell Mummy what was happening. But how do you explain something you don't fully understand?

One night, I cuddled up in Mummy's bed with her as she watched television, enjoying a rare break from her busy schedule. When I saw a couple on the television screen starting to French kiss, I pointed to the screen.

'That's how Uncle kisses me.'

Mummy turned her head. 'What?'

The fragile lilt in her voice told me that what I'd said was something important. I repeated my revelation in a whisper.

'That's how Uncle kisses me. And I don't like it. I don't like it at all.'

Mummy frowned at me. 'Are you sure?'

I nodded, but struggled to hold her gaze, wondering if I was about to get into trouble. Mummy stared at me, not saying a word for a few moments, then went back to watching television. I kept looking at her, confused about whether I should tell her more. I wanted to tell her about what Uncle did when he helped bathe me after school. I wanted to tell her about how my blue-tiled bathroom, the tiles on the walls and floor that went up the side of the sunken bathtub and into it, making the whole room a sea of blue right from the doorway of my bedroom, was now a place that terrified me.

Even when Uncle wasn't there, my bathroom always felt cold and scary. Even when I tried to hide from him, by lying on the cool, parquetry floor beneath my bed, as still and silent as the bed itself, he'd find me.

Uncle couldn't fit into that space. Down there, things were so different from what happened on the bed. But then, he would bend down to peer at me and softly tell me everything was going to be alright and reach his hands down to coax me out.

'Trust me, Liza. You're safe with me. Come out and I'll be gentle.'

His constant cooing of reassurances only stopped when he covered my mouth with his and shoved his tongue inside it.

I waited for Mummy to ask me something more about Uncle, wanting her to clear the confusion in my head and relieve me of my fears. Instead, she stayed silent. Now that I'd found a way to tell Mummy at least a little of what was happening, I hoped everything would be alright.

I tried not to think about the next time Mummy would have to leave us with the maids to travel interstate for a cooking show. But she did leave and, even though I was filled with a dread that Uncle might arrive and touch me that same way, alone in my bed, I never saw Uncle in our house again.

Nobody in my family ever spoke to me about the sexual abuse or told me that nobody had the right to touch me inappropriately. Life at home went on as it had before, as if nothing horrible had been taking place there for the last three years. Somehow, this strange silence made me wonder if it was me who had done something wrong. Was I to blame for what had happened? Nobody ever said I was, but they didn't tell me I wasn't either. I wished I'd revealed more to Mummy. But seeing her frown that day, I'd been too scared to, in case she got even more upset.

On TV, with her immaculately groomed hair, flawless make-up and authoritative chef voice, everyone saw my mother as a strong, confident woman. At home though, she cried a lot, no matter if the sun was shining brightly, the rose shrubs she'd planted in our front yard were in full bloom or even if I was cuddled up close to her. I knew she tried her best to hide her tears from Sharul and me, but we still saw her red eyes and stained cheeks and I couldn't understand why she seemed so constantly depressed. Daddy, on the other hand, was always wonderful to my brother and me and always smiling. Put Mummy and Daddy together, though and the furtive tension was painfully obvious.

I was too small to understand why they were always fighting. But I had already been taught that, when it came to adults, they weren't always what they seemed. They smiled when they were unhappy, lied about not hurting you, right before doing just that and they could convincingly play the role of the victim when caught out doing something wrong.

One day, not long after, I learnt we were expecting a guest for dinner. This was always exciting, given the flurry of activities in the kitchen and the extra prepping for dinner at such times, not to mention how Mummy enjoyed entertaining and basking in the compliments on her excellent cooking. But that day, she'd barely spoken to anyone, not even on the phone. The usual exuberance was missing.

I watched her in the kitchen as she silently went about preparing dinner.

'Who's coming for dinner, Mummy?'

Her reply was terse.

'One of Daddy's work colleagues.'

A little later, I was shocked to hear her sobbing on the phone, telling the person at the other end she wanted to end her life. When the doorbell rang, I followed Mummy to the front door. Daddy was already there, letting Norida in. She slipped her feet out of her shoes and stepped across the threshold.

Mummy didn't welcome Norida with open arms the way she usually greeted her guests. And she didn't smile all through dinner, either. Not even once. Very few words were exchanged between the three of them, Mummy, Daddy and Norida, but I could feel something wasn't right.

In her simple, blue, cotton baju kurung and tudung, Norida looked dowdy next to Mummy in her silken kebaya embroidered with gold thread. Cobalt blue eyeliner highlighted Mummy's eyes, pale pink lipstick accentuated her mouth. And despite her sadness, there was a faint glow of pride on her face and understated elegance in her bearing. The plain-looking Norida wore no make-up. She stood nervously before us. In contrast, Daddy seemed pleased with himself. He was the only one who seemed to be genuinely smiling.

I didn't see Norida again, but things changed in our home after that night. We still went to the Commonwealth Club and had fun together as a family, but the "all is well" atmosphere my parents tried to create, seemed suddenly fake. It felt like I had just seen the curtain pulled back to reveal the reality of a magician's trick and I could never look at it again the same way.

One day, I heard Mummy and Daddy screaming at each other downstairs. Mummy's voice was high-pitched and desperate. Daddy yelled back. The sudden crash of breaking porcelain sent me scurrying down the stairs to the lounge room to find Mummy smashing her beautiful dolls on the floor, one by one. I stood by the television set, scared stiff, watching her scream as she destroyed these treasures she had once loved so much.

When she finished smashing them all, Mummy dropped to her knees and started pulling at her hair.

'I'll kill myself. Or why don't you just kill me yourself? I don't want to live like this.'

Daddy was as still as a statue for a few moments. Then he turned and left the room.

I looked at the remnants of dolls scattered across the floor, then at Mummy. One day she's going to kill herself. One day I'm going to wake up and find Mummy dead. The thought terrified me. She was my everything.

After Daddy left, my maid took me away to get bathed and dressed. When I returned to the lounge room, it was tidy again. No one mentioned the dolls or the argument again. In the same way other unpleasant events in our house had been swept away, out of sight and mind, life went back to its normal routine as if nothing had happened.

A few years later, while Mummy was away on a photo shoot in the Philippines, Daddy brought Norida to our house again. He had a beautiful rag doll for me when they arrived. Some could've considered her black bead eyes, fabric-covered button nose and large magenta smile as ugly. But I adored her. I named her Lamia and from that day onwards, she became my confidant and most treasured possession. When I proudly showed Lamia to Mummy after she returned home, my mother's brows puckered as she asked how I'd got her.

'Daddy and his friend gave her to me,' I said.

Mummy just pressed her lips together, not saying or asking anything else about Lamia. In the days that followed, instead of finding her in a tearful, despondent mood at home, I often detected a grim, determined look on her face. Something had changed, but I'd no idea what. Then, Mummy and Daddy made a startling announcement. We were moving to Australia.

I asked how far away Australia was and Daddy told me it was across the ocean from us. When Mummy kissed me goodnight that evening, something had transformed her. She looked triumphant. I was barely 10, but I was old enough to realise this move was to save their marriage.

After Mummy left the room, I clutched Lamia to my chest and stroked her woollen hair.

'It's okay, Lamia,' I said, 'think of it as a holiday. We'll see lots of kangaroos and koalas and strawberries too. Lots of them. It'll be just like visiting Strawberry Shortcake land.'

I didn't know it then, but in truth, I was trying to reassure myself. I traced my finger around Lamia's permanent smile and wished I could always be happy, like she was.

On the day of our departure, our entire family, grandparents, aunts, uncles and cousins and a large group, came to see us off. It was as if there was a party at the airport, except that everyone was crying. I knew nothing could be changed now, but still, I begged and pleaded with Mummy and Daddy to change their minds. Of course, they didn't and I lost every shred of hope I'd been holding on to until then.

In Melbourne, Daddy soon settled into his new job at a hospital in the city and with Mummy not working, Sharul and I got all her attention. By the time we bought our first house, I had begun to enjoy our new life in Australia.

Mummy planted a crab apple tree, the closest she could find to the Ceri Kampung with its sweet cherry-like fruit, and roses, just like we had in our garden in Malaysia. But the most wonderful thing I loved about our yard was when the grass grew long. It was soft and lush. I'd lay in it and swish my arms back and forth, flattening the grass beneath my limbs into a grass angel, and gazing up at the animal-shaped clouds rolling by.

When Mummy told us she was pregnant, I didn't understand what she meant. Even when her tummy started to grow, I still didn't realise there was a new baby on the way. And when she delivered, it really did seem as if she quickly went from telling us she was pregnant, to having a larger belly and then coming home from the hospital with a new baby brother for me. Right from the start, I loved helping change Dane's nappies and playing with him every opportunity I got.

By the time I started year eight, after having trouble fitting into two public high schools, I was enrolled into a private college for girls. At both the earlier schools, I'd been the only dark-skinned student in the class and though not exactly bullied, I was often referred to as the Aboriginal, making me feel isolated and insecure. I'd developed a shyness that prevented me from making any close friends. It was the same at my new school as well. I'd no idea how to blend in with my classmates.

But there was one wealthy Asian girl, Jocelyn, who was hugely popular and showed an interest in me. I'd never seen anyone bust a move on the dance floor like her. We didn't hang out together at school during the day but after school we talked about fashion and our dreams for the future. To me, her friendship felt genuine.

I missed my extended family in Malaysia though, especially my cousin Naznina and Aunty Aish. Frequent long-distance phone calls helped bridge the distance between us. No one realised the calls were all reverse charge until a big, fat bill arrived at Naznina's house.

It was huge compared to the small amount on the shopping receipt Mummy found in the pocket of Daddy's work pants one day when she was doing the washing. It was from a mall in Preston, a locality unfamiliar to us. The items on the list were things we never used and Daddy hadn't brought them home, either.

Mummy questioned Daddy about the receipt as soon as he returned from work. He seemed to be shocked. But she wasn't convinced. She decided to investigate things on her own, beginning with a call to the hospital where Daddy worked. She discovered that Norida had arrived in Australia not long after we had four years earlier and she was working at the hospital with Daddy. Worse still, she now had a child.

I was upset and angry too. I thought of all the times I'd waited up each Saturday night so I could cook egg soufflé for Daddy after he got home from work at around 3 am. I had no idea he was coming home late because he was spending time with Norida at her house. I'd never blamed my father, even when I first suspected his involvement with Norida. I was in year nine at school now and at 14, he was still my hero. I directed my fury towards Norida. In my eyes, she was an evil homewrecker. At home, Daddy continued to lie.

'I don't care about Norida, she's nothing to me. I love only you.'

But Mummy had endured enough. She'd agreed to leave her family, a successful career and the home she loved, to save her marriage. And now it was clear her husband had not made the same sacrifices. She needed time out and returned to Malaysia with Dane and me, so she could decide what she wanted to do next.

Back in Malaysia, I was thrilled to reunite with my first cousin, Azahar, and his older brother, Maleek. Maleek, who was 19 and studying in America, was home on vacation, making the family gathering even more special. It felt cool hanging out with an older cousin. Mummy didn't mind me spending so much time with the boys. She felt especially close to them, since their mother, her sister, Sabrina, had passed away.

One day, Maleek invited me to join him and Azahar for a night out. At first, Mummy objected but it was mainly because Amma, my maternal grandmother, was living at our house then.

'Are you mad? And what will Amma think? How can I let you come in late at night?'

Mummy knew my grandmother would disapprove. I remembered her telling me how Amma had punished her for sneaking out to meet Daddy before they were married. Amma tied her to a tree and poured honey over her legs so the red ants would bite her. I knew Mummy would never do something like that to me and she wouldn't let Amma do it either. But I also knew, even as an adult, going against Amma's wishes was hard for her.

For Mummy, being religious wasn't the issue. With her troubled marriage already the talk of the town, she didn't want everyone also saying she was a bad mother, not bothered about disciplining her 14-year-old daughter.

I saw the temptation of a fun night slipping away from me and pleaded with her to let me spend time with my cousins. It was only after she talked to Aunty Hanees, her best friend and my godmother, that she relented.

'Let her go,' Aunty Hanees told her. 'She'll be with her cousins. Who better for her to go out with, than her family?'

And that was how I finally walked into a bar at 11:30 that Saturday night, accompanied by Azahar and Maleek. I'd been to under-age discos in Australia, but it was just crowds of kids packed into a dark room with loud music. Here, it felt like I was about to enter the adult scene.

Maleek offered me a drink, but I declined. There is no limit on the drinking age in Malaysia. You just must be over 18 to buy it. I didn't need alcohol anyway; music and dancing were all the intoxication I needed. But the bar we were at, turned out to be downright boring. Hardly anyone was dancing.

At around one in the morning, we went to one of the many crowded night stalls in Malaysia. We ordered Tandoori chicken. Up until that moment, everything felt fine. Then Maleek asked me which part of the chicken I wanted to eat. Looking at me intently, he said, 'Breast?'

Something about his tone seemed different. I felt awkward but pushed the feeling aside. So many people ignore these moments of realisation and intuition. For me, the consequences were about to be devastating.

Around 2 am, instead of returning to my house, I went back to theirs for the night. It solved the problem of Amma being disturbed and disapproving of my night out. Azahar was going to watch DVDs in his room upstairs and Maleek declared he was going to watch Indecent Proposal in his room downstairs. The movie had only just been released and I wanted to see it too. So, while Azahar went to his room, Maleek and I lay on his bed and watched together.

I fell asleep sometime during the movie and woke up with a start to find Maleek on top of me, rubbing his naked crotch against me. The unwelcome feeling of his hands on my body took me back to those still, quiet moments under my bed on that cool, parquetry flooring. But this time I had no doubt that what was happening to me was wrong.

'No, no. Please, Anne, please, Brother.'

Maleek's body was pinning me down and I could barely move as he tried to pull my pants down.

'No, Maleek, please stop!'

He struggled to control my frantic efforts to push him away and continued to abuse me until he ejaculated on my thighs. I didn't even know that boys ejaculated. Suddenly, Azahar was knocking on the door.

'What are you guys doing? Open the door.'

As soon as Maleek moved off me, I leapt from the bed. I felt the nausea rise within my belly and rushed to the bathroom. I sobbed as I washed myself, then went upstairs to Azahar's bedroom.

'I want to go home. I want to go home – now!'

Neither of us spoke in the car when Azahar drove me home. It was only a 10-minute trip, but it felt like hours. I couldn't wait to reach the safety of my own house. When I opened the door to let myself in, Mummy greeted me with a tight hug. She'd waited up all night for me and was relieved I was finally back home.

'Oh, Liza, I was so worried something had happened to you.'

I couldn't bring myself to tell her that her worries were founded. And at that moment, I felt what had happened was all my fault. I showered before going to bed but couldn't wash away the disgust that I felt. Had the tartan pants I'd worn that night been inappropriate? Were they too tight? Had I led Maleek on in any way? The movie I'd watched, laying on his bed, was that wrong? My neck and chest felt tight.

I wished I could dive into a swimming pool and feel happy and free and clean again. But I knew no amount of water could wash away the guilt in my mind. Now, I know that a victim should never be blamed for the abuse they suffer. But how could I have figured this out at 14 on my own?

I was relieved to find an opportunity to reveal everything to Aunty Hanees a little later in the day when she took me for an outing to a luxurious resort, along with her family.

'Something happened…' I said.

The expression on her face changed from curiosity to confusion as she listened to me. Then she disappeared into the resort. I assumed she was calling Mummy. But after that, neither Aunty Hanees, nor Mummy later at home, spoke anything about what had happened to me.

I'd been worried that learning about Maleek abusing me, would plunge Mummy into the depths of anguish. Instead, I found her and everyone else doing what they always did and life went on as usual, as if no one had heard a word of what I'd confessed. No one spoke directly to me about it and I didn't know if they knew the truth or if anyone had spoken to Maleek to reprimand him.

The strange silence from Mummy and other close relatives added to my burden of guilt. And after being excited and eager to visit Malaysia, all I wanted to do now was return to Australia. Maleek, on the other hand, taunted me at every opportunity he got. When we met at any common relative's place, he would deliberately block my path until I softly asked him to let me pass. When we went for family dinners, he would sit opposite me, stick his foot under the table and slide it up my skirt. During those last two weeks in Malaysia, with no one making any attempt to support me or even console me, I became increasingly withdrawn and depressed.

Two days before we were due to leave Malaysia, Maleek cornered me in a room and I had my chance to confront him.

'I trusted you. I didn't expect you to take advantage of me.'

The arrogance in his voice was unsettling.

'You wanted it.'

I was too stunned to respond. To make matters worse, he coolly added that he had feelings for me. I felt my head spinning.

He was a close relative, my first cousin. Couldn't he see how wrong his thinking was?

On the flight home, I wrote him a letter about how I didn't like what he'd done to me. I trusted him as a brother. But he was trying to make me feel I should look at him in a different way. I handed the letter to the air hostess, so it would be carried back to Malaysia on the plane and reach Maleek soon after I arrived in Australia.

On our third night back in Melbourne, the phone rang at 2 am. I knew as soon as it rang, that something terrible had happened. Mummy's voice sounded frantic.

'Oh, no, I'm so sorry. I can't believe this myself. Don't worry. I'll handle it.'

I then heard Daddy saying similar things. Minutes later, they both came to my bedroom. Daddy dragged me from my bed.

'How could you do this?' He was yelling and began slapping me across the shoulders and back. 'You've brought such shame on us!'

Maleek had obviously feared that, once I was home in Australia, I might disclose what he'd done. To cut that possibility off, he'd shown my letter to my aunties and uncles, telling them I obviously had feelings for him. I curled myself into a ball and covered my face with my hands, even as Daddy kept hitting me.

'Maleek is lying. It wasn't my fault.'

My tears were hot, fat drops on my face. But neither of them believed me. Daddy's blows rained down on me until Mummy had to force herself between us to stop him hitting me.

'Enough!'

After they left my room, I climbed back into bed and cried myself to sleep. That day, Daddy's attitude toward me shifted. He took to calling me a prostitute and even started looking at me as if

I really was one. It felt like even Mummy had turned against me. I realised our entire family in Malaysia was talking about what a horrible girl I was. Mummy had been forced to choose between a nephew, who'd always treated her with the utmost respect, and a daughter that everyone said was only pretending to be innocent.

The two people I loved and trusted more than anyone else, chose to believe the perpetrator of the crime over the victim – their own daughter. My spirit died a painful, gory death. I felt abandoned.

As the horror of being abused, first by my uncle and then by my cousin, began to sink in, the self-loathing followed. I focused on the idea that I was unclean and impure. And with no one showing concern about what I'd gone through, I began to feel worthless as well. At 14, it was too much for my young mind to take. I couldn't make sense of the pain inflicted on me by my own relatives.

Why me?

DROWNING IN DESPAIR

Forgive yourself, and then take the step forward.

1990 - 1992

As you learn and evolve, long before acceptance and deeper understanding, reflection can be less productive and is more just an endless movie loop on replay that reminds you of your trauma and despair. That's where I was… then.

Towards the end of that year, I started acting up in school and stealing things, petty things, on impulse, from the other girls. It's something I'll always feel deeply ashamed of. But at that time, caring enough about myself to feel ashamed wasn't part of my mindset. Instead, I was a void. A blankness.

I felt lost, unhappy and confused about why I'd stolen things I didn't need in the first place. My parents were well-off, so I certainly wasn't lacking any ability to surround myself with "stuff". All I knew was, I resented the other girls who I believed led uncomplicated lives and had loving families.

When the fees for the private school I'd been enrolled in, with such pride and ambition, became too steep for the reality of my parents' financial situation, they decided to get me admitted into a public school for Year 10. I suppose that, from their perspective, paying hefty school fees for an education that they believed I was disrespecting and not making the most of, must have seemed like wasted money. The only thing I knew I would miss about the private school was Jocelyn. Luckily, we found a way of keeping in touch. I did manage to make a couple of good friends in the new school and this helped me settle in initially. However, it didn't prevent suicidal thoughts from sneaking into my vulnerable young mind.

Each time my father looked at me with his undisguised revulsion, I slipped even deeper into the darkness of loneliness and despair. It pained me that his attitude towards me was so terribly unfair, considering I hadn't done anything wrong, other than to react and act out as a direct result of the wrongs that had been done to me.

Looking back on the ways we become the people we are, can sometimes be a powerful learning tool. Other times, it can lend itself to wallowing self-pity. In those terrible times, when I was knee-deep in parental disappointment, judgement and emotional isolation, I started to think back to the time when my uncle used to molest me.

At that time, both my father and mother had overlooked the most primal needs I had. I simply wanted to be reassured and consoled. Nurtured. Protected. I didn't understand what was being done to me and when they were unable to even attempt to find the courage to confront my molester and shame him, the message that their behaviour sent me was that I didn't matter. And what was worse was the all-encompassing notion I had brought shame on our family.

They were firmly pointing a finger of accusation at me. I wondered what stopped them from putting their arms around me instead. I waited for them to believe in me and offer support. To tell me: We can work through this together. We'll stand by you.

I waited forever.

I was nothing but a worthless, trouble-making teenage

daughter. I was someone they had every right to feel ashamed of. Those thoughts consumed me and crowded my mind. But I didn't have the strength to fight back. What was the point? Nobody ever seemed to believe me.

Mummy's dramatic displays from childhood had trained me in the art of suicidal thoughts and now they swirled inside my head. I decided there was only one logical way out for me. Of course, it wasn't logical at all. But if my mother's actions had taught me anything, it was to get it right and not just talk about it. If I wanted out of that endless pain, I needed to get the job done properly.

I remembered being told that liquid paper, white-out correction fluid, was dangerous and incredibly toxic. I immediately got hold of a couple of bottles. The night I decided to end my life, I retrieved them from their spot in my desk and scanned the room for something else that would add to my weaponry.

What exactly I was looking for, wasn't clear to me, but I felt that the white-out on its own wouldn't be enough. I grabbed a pair of my stockings from one of my drawers and pictured strangling myself for added effect, while inhaling the chemicals. It would be painless, I was sure. I decided I would also slip a pillowcase over my head to ensure there were more fumes than oxygen going up my nose. Just in case. My deathly stage was set.

With a bottle stuck up each of my nostrils and the pillowcase covering my head, the effect of the fumes was almost instant. I felt like I was choking. I pulled on the ends of the stockings to further tighten the knot I'd made around my neck and focused on this action to overcome my body's survival instinct to remove itself from the cause of harm. I was determined.

It didn't take long before sharp pains started stabbing through my head. I felt as if knitting needles were being shoved up my nostrils and I started gasping for air. Suddenly, I realised this wasn't the way I wanted to die. I lacked the courage to deal with the pain of dying. Why couldn't self-inflicted death be peaceful and painless?

The disappointment of botching this critical mission I'd set for myself was more than I could bear. I pulled the pillowcase off my head, untangled the stockings from around my neck and removed the liquid paper bottles from my nostrils, before curling up like an unborn baby, still in the womb. The hot tears stung my eyes. I was such a failure. I had not succeeded at living, but I couldn't even stop living, either. The days and months wiggled on relentlessly.

I managed to keep my first attempt at suicide from my parents, but after just a few weeks at yet another new school they decided to send me to for year 11, I made a second attempt at taking my life.

This time, it was Panadol – a full pack. For someone who couldn't stand the sight of blood and slitting my wrists, it seemed like a good option. But dozens of tablets later, a pounding headache and the urgent need to vomit, put an end to another life-ending plan.

My second failure pushed me deeper into depression, but nobody noticed. Or, if they did, they didn't do anything to deal with it. I'm not sure which scenario makes me sadder. At home, Daddy always seemed mad at me and often disappointed with Sharul as well. I wondered why he even bothered coming home.

One night, while we were having dinner, the sight of me seemed to frustrate him so much, he sprang to his feet and upturned the table, without a single care about the mess he left for someone else to clean up. My fear of him was growing and I stayed out of his way as much as possible.

I was no longer the little girl who adored him and he was no longer the doting father. It was all gone. Lost forever. My anxiety levels reached new levels and triggered recurring panic attacks. Any shred of the once happy, loved, secure child was now lost, too. My new perceptions of loveless mistrust shadowed every step I took.

At the new public school, I kept mostly to myself but felt drawn to Melissa. Despite what I saw as pretty poise and a genuine comfort with who she was, she seemed to only have a few close friends and happily welcomed me into her world. It was usual kid stuff: riding bikes, flying kites, laughing. But she had wisdom and empathy beyond the kids I had known and when I confided in her about what my cousin Maleek had done two years before, she bluntly told me that it was rape.

Rape? I had to ask her what that was. I knew what Maleek had done was wrong, but even in Year 11, I still didn't know a crime like that had a name. I was that naïve. It was also the first time anyone had explicitly told me I wasn't the one who should feel guilty about what had happened. That guilt, Melissa told me, lay solely with Maleek.

The clarity it gave me should have felt refreshing, I guess, but the realisation the event that had taken place truly was serious and a crime, seemed to only add to my sense of hopelessness. Apart from Melissa and Jocelyn, who called me occasionally, there was no-one either at home or at school who I felt comfortable enough with to share my deepest thoughts. All I could think of was escaping from the pain and ridding myself of these crushing feelings of despair.

Then one night, I planned what I believed would be my final suicide attempt. I'd put my plan into action in the morning. And this time, I told myself, I'd succeed.

It was the weekend and everyone was home that morning,

busy avoiding the truth of their lives. For what felt like the thousandth time, I wondered why Daddy didn't admit he was unhappy in this marriage and opt out, instead of behaving like he was forced to continue living with us. And why didn't Mummy stand up for herself and leave him instead of putting all her energy into keeping up appearances of a happy marriage? All of us knew about Daddy having an affair with Norida. Yet, when he denied the affair repeatedly, we acted as though we believed him, as a show of family loyalty. So, why didn't they believe me? The whole situation felt unbearable.

I waited until everyone had finished breakfast and showered and dressed for the day and then, taking a tall empty glass with me, locked myself in the bathroom. I turned on the shower to mask the noise of the bathroom cupboard door opening and closing again as I reached for the bottle of cleaning products we stored beneath the vanity unit.

I opened a half-full bottle of the household liquid bleach, White King. A bitter lemon smell stung my nostrils as I filled a quarter of the glass with it. I added Spray and Wipe, squeezed a thick stream of JIF cream over this and topped the glass up with Dettol. I mixed the concoction using the handle of a toothbrush that I then carefully washed and put back in its holder. I didn't want to poison anyone else.

I started gulping down the lethal cocktail. It was warm and tasted horribly bitter. I couldn't get past four gulps. I started to retch. I set the glass on the bench and dropped to the wet floor, foaming at the mouth, choking and gasping for breath. The hot steam from the shower added to my feeling of suffocation. Was I going to die here on the tiles? I panicked, dragged myself to the door and began to fumble with the knob. I crawled out of the steamy bathroom and down the hallway hoping someone would see me and help.

The sound of a scream pierced the air. It was my cousin, June, who was staying with us. Then Mummy was by my side and I could hear the sound of her guttural sobs. Sharul heard the commotion and was trying to pour milk down my throat when my father arrived. He snatched a knife from the kitchen knife block and held it against my throat as he screamed at me.

'You want to kill yourself? I'll do it for you.'

I wanted to tell him that I no longer wanted to die but the poisons had taken my voice.

Mummy was still crying loudly and Sharul looked distraught as he pushed my father aside.

'Go away!'

My guilt for doing this to my family was overwhelming. They were having a quiet morning and I'd ruined it. My insides were burning and I couldn't squeeze out even a few words to tell them how sorry I was. I started vomiting up the milk. My throat felt like it was ablaze again as the hot mix of poisons followed in violent bursts from my mouth.

When I regained consciousness, I was in the darkness of my parents' bedroom, with the curtains drawn tight against the remaining daylight. I could hear the whispers of my parents' voices nearby and I realised they'd decided not to take me to the doctor. Instead, they'd tucked me into bed to rest. Perhaps, they were scared they'd get into trouble.

When they realised I'd woken up, Mummy gave me a relieved smile and brought me a platter of finger sandwiches and some juice. Before she left the room, she patted me on the head and said, 'I love you so much, Liza. Please don't frighten us like this again.'

Daddy sat on the bed by my side. I could see the glint of tears in his eyes.

'Tell me, Liza,' he said calmly, 'what can I do to stop you from ever doing something like this again?'

I felt I could see the love I'd craved for so long in his eyes again.

'What can I do, Liza?' Daddy said again.

My voice was low and steady.

'Just please tell me that you believe me,' I replied. 'And promise me you'll ring up Maleek and Uncle Tajudeen and tell them you believe me.'

'Yes, Liza, I will,' Daddy said. 'If that's what you want, I'll do it.'

But he never made those calls. Like so many other unpleasant happenings in my life, this one was also given a quiet burial. My physical body recovered quickly, although my emotional state of anxiety and stress worsened. As a coping mechanism, I got into the habit of skipping my school's year 12 classes and taking a tram to the city whenever I felt like it.

As I strolled down Collins Street, I'd forget about being considered a troublemaking liar and a shame to my family. I'd walk past eye-catching boutique windows with anorexic mannequins draped in sexy designer gowns and fake gems. At the end of the block, I'd turn right and head for the one shopfront that attracted me the most - the magnificent Chanel store.

The chic, conservative styling resonated strongly with my religious upbringing. But most of all, it was the sense of empowerment the outfits exuded that held me spellbound. I knew this was the kind of store where I'd want to shop. Visions of myself as a powerful businesswoman, dressed in a Chanel outfit, a Chanel handbag on my arm, sashaying into an expensive restaurant or designer boutique where other people turned their heads to look at me, would race through my mind. And then I'd crash back into the real world. I would never be able to shop there.

A feeling of deep frustration came over me every time I gazed into that shop window. I comforted myself with the idea that, although it wasn't my reality now, it could be one day. Someday I'll walk into that store like a VIP shopper and they will all know my name.

Eventually, I had to return to my family. Each time I stepped back on the tram, all I was running away from would wind itself around me like a spider trapping its prey inside its web. It wasn't long before the school principal wanted to know why I wasn't attending classes. So, I wrote a letter, supposedly from my parents, saying I hadn't been well and had to stay home from school.

Not long after, I was called out of science class and asked to go to the principal's office. My heart started thumping even faster when I found my parents sitting there with the principal. Their three grim faces told me I was in big trouble.

The principal held out the letter I'd forged and asked if I was responsible for it. As I stared at the handwritten letter he waved in my face, I realised I'd focused so much on perfecting my parents' signatures, I'd forgotten to change my handwriting when I wrote it. I had no option but to own up to what I'd been doing when I should've been in school. Strangely, once we got home, my parents didn't berate me for the forgery. But I knew the incident had reinforced my father's belief that I couldn't be trusted. And though Mummy looked shocked and hurt that I could be so deceitful, she seemed more concerned about me going to the city on my own and putting myself at risk from all the dangers she believed lurked there. I found that ironic. She was always worried about my physical safety, but the harm I'd suffered until then had all come from homegrown sources: my father, uncle and cousin.

Skipping school obviously now had to stop. But it was the one excitement that was keeping me alive. I told my parents another lie: that I wanted to join a study group at the State Library in the city on Saturdays. There was no "study group" but it wasn't a total fabrication. Every Saturday I did go to the State Library. It was a golden time for me, with most of it spent in the grandeur of the La Trobe Reading Room, admiring its soaring, high-domed, octagonal ceiling, huge wooden desks, and chunky heritage chairs.

I didn't do much reading, though occasionally I'd flip through the pages of a book that caught my fancy. Most of the time, I'd sit at a desk, doodling on paper, immersed in daydreams. I'd imagine myself growing up to be a successful doctor or lawyer and winning the trust and respect of my family. But each time I walked out of the library, the miserable reality of my life would hit me and the despair would take over. The darkness inside me intensified even further, sucking me into a mineshaft of wretchedness. Then suddenly, someone threw me a lifeline and helped me claw my way out.

RUNNING AWAY

1993-1994

The school counsellor, my school forced me to see, turned out to be an empathetic gentleman who seemed genuinely concerned about me. He told me I had options and I could legally leave home with the help of government financial support. The wheels were set in motion quickly.

Jocelyn's offer of support strengthened my determination to leave home. It wasn't long after that, Mummy announced she was going to Malaysia for a week. I decided to run away soon after she left.

The moment I returned home from the airport with Daddy and Sharul, after seeing Mummy off, I got busy packing a few clothes, books and other personal stuff I thought I'd need. The next morning, I waited till Daddy left for work to call for a taxi and watched nervously as a few minutes later it slowed to a halt outside my house. I loaded my bags and boxes into the boot and collapsed into the backseat.

I left with a lot of pain in my heart. But I also took something else I had no right to take. My pocket was heavy with a gold necklace I'd taken from Mummy's jewellery box. It was worth a lot of money, money I felt I just might need to tide me through the first few weeks of living on my own and perhaps, in the event of an emergency.

In the beginning, Jocelyn and her lovely family invited me

to temporarily share their home — a sprawling house with a tennis court and a pool with a huge waterfall in the middle of it. Jocelyn's parents were the kindest people I'd ever met. How I wished my parents were like them. I looked at Jocelyn. Her happy face said it all. She was living the dream. A solid family, a solid home, a solid life.

The guilt I felt about hurting my family prompted a phone call to Daddy a few days later.

He pleaded with me to come home and tried his best to convince me to return. But now I'd tasted the freedom of being on my own, I wasn't ready to comply. There was another teary phone call, this time with Mummy, but I was committed.

I soon enrolled to complete my year 12 studies at a senior secondary college in Hawthorn, just across the road from Swinburne University. When an advertisement for local share accommodation at $60 a week appeared on the uni noticeboard, I sold Mummy's gold necklace, for much less than it was worth, and moved in there with an Asian student and his sister. They already occupied a bedroom each in the two-bedroom apartment, so I was offered the lounge room. To my mind, I had the better end of the bargain.

I quickly fell into a routine of sorts. I attended my classes but, instead of trying to make friends at the school, I spent each lunch hour in the university library on the other side of the road. I had Jocelyn and I liked hanging out with the older tertiary students who seemed so self-assured and independent. Many of them were international students from India and Malaysia and the familiarity of their faces made it feel like home.

Joining the Indian Association Club connected me to their community in a way that felt meaningful and fun. Beneath the surface, though, I couldn't deny the guilt I felt about enjoying living away from home on my own when my parents were eager for me to come back to them.

Then, I met Gaz.

His fair skin was a product of his Indian/Anglo heritage and, combined with his dark, slightly dishevelled hair, I found it hard to take my eyes off him. He stared back. It was as if he'd cast an invisible lasso around me and drawn me in. I didn't think I'd ever see him again. I was wrong.

A few days later, I was flattered at being considered pretty enough to be asked to participate in the Indian Society's show at the uni. The schedule of events kicked off with traditional Indian dance performances, followed by an Indian dress fashion show. I happily attended the practice sessions but, on the day of the event, it was harder to hide my nervousness. I tried my best to strut with something resembling confidence and it helped that I was decked out in a beautiful ghagra choli – a dress mostly worn by Indian brides. I'd never heard so many people talk about me in such a positive way before and it made me feel ... special. I left the stage on a high and caught sight of the same Anglo-Indian guy, clapping enthusiastically in the audience. Just like they had in the library only a few days before, our eyes met and, for a moment, time seemed to stand still again.

When I quizzed a friend about who this mystery man was, I found out his name was Gaz and he was studying engineering. The idea of talking to him myself seemed terrifying, so I asked my friend to pass on a message from me to tell Gaz I thought he was cute.

I'd almost finished getting back into my regular clothes when there was a knock on the change room door. I opened it to find Gaz there. We introduced ourselves and then he asked if I'd like to grab a bite to eat at the McDonald's nearby. I couldn't believe

I was out on a date with him. I knew many of the girls from the Indian Society would surely think he was hot and want to be with him. But here he was sitting at McDonalds with *me*! By the time we finished our food, Gaz had asked me on another date and I'd given him my parents' home number.

Over the next few weeks, I returned to the home of my parents for occasional weekend meals that reinforced my determination to live away from them. There were many things I missed about them, but I'd been missing them for so many years before I left, anyway. And now that I had Gaz interested in me, an emotional hole had been filled. I was where I was meant to be, or so I thought.

It wasn't long before our budding romance progressed even further and we made love. The experience wasn't all about fireworks or euphoria. It was basically something I felt I needed to do. For me, sex wasn't something you had with just anyone. It invariably brought back memories of things being done to my body in the past. Today, I know it was natural for me to feel that way. According to psychiatrists specialised in treating sexually assault victims, no matter how long ago the assault has taken place, the experience can change the way such survivors experience sex. For some, sexual intimacy could also trigger distressing memories.

My first meeting with Gaz's parents took place at his father's grand 60th birthday party. That day, I took Jocelyn along with me for moral support. I could see Gaz's folks loved him deeply, but they also seemed very prim and proper. His mum, a stylishly dressed, fair-skinned Indian, spoke to me politely, but her tone was cold. Her conversation with me was more like an impersonal interrogation.

'You've left home? What do your parents do? What are you

studying?' In contrast, Gaz's dad had a warm smile and seemed more welcoming.

After that first visit to his house, I couldn't wait to marry Gaz. I was just 17, but already eager to be his wife. In my mind, as an Asian with a Malaysian-Indian background, I had done something outrageously improper by running away from home. I naïvely believed getting married would set my life back on the right course.

In the culture I come from, girls are groomed to believe that marriage is the answer to life's every problem. Just get married and have kids and everything will be fine! That's what is drummed into our heads from the moment we become adolescents. Besides, being made to believe I was ugly and drab, I was thrilled that someone as handsome as Gaz was interested in me, which made me feel even more desperate to get married to him and have a family. A family that would love me, protect me and fight for me. Maybe, Gaz's family could do all that for me…

His parents didn't seem too enthused about me or our relationship, but they didn't seem overly worried either. Of course, I'm sure they never thought Gaz would want to marry me. After all, I was a runaway and followed a different religion and their bright and handsome son was a future engineer with, what they must have hoped, would be a wonderful future.

TOXIC LOVE

1994-1996

Every weekend, Gaz would pick up Jocelyn and me in his hatchback red car and we'd go clubbing. I was convinced we were deeply in love, so when Gaz showed signs of control and jealousy, I ignored them, even when those signs became physical. I was a 17-year-old who'd been trained to believe that, when things went wrong, it must be my fault. Now I blamed myself for making Gaz feel jealous.

Before long, Gaz began to hit me for the most trivial reasons. Sometimes, for no reason at all. He would pinch me or squeeze my hand so tight that it felt like my fingers would break. It never crossed my mind that no one had the right to treat me like that, even if I'd made them angry. We all have voices in our head and mine kept telling me I was worthless in every way.

No matter how much abuse he dished out, choosing to think about the few positive moments that still existed between us meant I was always able to see positives about him, including the way he seemed intent on helping me mend my relationship with my mother.

When Mummy enrolled for a short university course related to counselling, 'So I can understand how to help you,' she'd told me, Gaz drove me to the university building every Tuesday so I could spend time with her. His vicious streak was undeniable, but my skewed outlook meant I still saw him as a caring and wonderful boyfriend. Then things got worse.

Gaz became jealous and angry, even if men simply looked at me while we were out together. His angry pinches and squeezing of my skin turned to violent slaps. The night he smashed his fist into my face, after accusing me of flirting with another man, ended with me needing surgery and a metal plate inserted to support my damaged eye socket and cheekbone.

The incision for inserting the metal plate had been made above my hairline, so the scar from the stitches wouldn't be seen once my hair grew back. Although the surgery went well, I was convinced my face would be even uglier than I already imagined it was. The surgeon was pleased with the end result, though. A couple of days later, when he came to check how well I was healing, he gave Gaz a grim stare and said to me, 'The next time, if whoever did this to you does it again, he'll go to jail for a very long time.'

But I didn't want that. I loved Gaz too much. I didn't want to ruin his career. I just wanted him to stop hurting me. My stomach had churned at the first glimpse of what he'd done to my face. A part of me wanted to report him to the police. But it was just a fleeting thought. I didn't have the heart to do that.

After the surgery, I couldn't chew properly for a long time and had to eat through a straw. When Gaz visited me every day while I was in hospital, to help me manage my food, it felt like he was once again giving me the love I craved so much. I stopped thinking about how he was the reason I needed help and only focused on the help he was giving me and how kind I thought that was.

Once I was healed, Gaz went back to clubbing and his old habits of coming back to my place afterwards, drunk and boisterous and wanting sex. I didn't refuse him, even though the love-making was rough and mechanical.

Just the fact he'd come to see me, made me feel reassured.

I believed that, somewhere inside of him, he cared for me, he needed me and he badly wanted to be with me. The stories we tell ourselves can be so powerful. Thinking back to that time today, I can see what was really going on inside Gaz's head then. He'd been trying to make sure I believed he still loved me so I wouldn't tell anyone the truth about my broken face.

The night he repeatedly kicked me in the stomach in a nightclub carpark, for what he saw as some other supposed indiscretion, shocked me into taking a good friend's advice and applying for a restraining order. I surprised myself by actually going through with it but, in the weeks after the police had served it on him, and Gaz asked me how I could have done such a thing to him, I agreed to try again and I took him back.

It was a terrible mistake. My decision to let him back into my life, even after his extreme violence towards me, seemed to strengthen his power over me. He alternated between humiliating me in public, to sharing loving, caring moments with me at my apartment at night. I so badly wanted to be loved, to belong, that I didn't realise holding the door open to Gaz was inviting more pain and isolation into my life.

As I prepared to sit my year 12 exams, the pressure of missing my family, living week-to-week on the tight budget of my Centrelink benefits and the abuse from Gaz, soon took its toll.

One morning, I waited until my roommates left and swallowed four packets of Panadol. I curled up in a ball and waited for death to come and get me. Instead of death, a friend, who had called to have a chat, found me slurring my words and recognised something was wrong. When I woke up in a hospital bed with a drip in my arm and the gritty taste of the vomit-inducing charcoal drink they'd fed me, still on my tongue, the reality of my depression kicked in.

By the time I came out of the hospital, I'd missed my year 12 exams. This meant my final year was officially unscored and my dreams of getting high enough marks to study medicine or law were shattered. I was heartbroken, but I was also determined to be a survivor and it wasn't long before my entrepreneurial spirit kicked in.

With my Centrelink payments coming in regularly and the time I spent babysitting and promoting the club on Friday nights, pulling in some additional funds, I had enough to launch a small business of my own.

My mother had many flaws and failings, but she was an amazing cook. Growing up, watching her cookery shows on TV, had taught me some impressive skills and helped me find a welcome escape in cooking. So, when I was ready to start my own entrepreneurial venture, choosing something related to food seemed like an ideal fit.

I decided to begin with two types of meal packages. One vegetarian curry with rice; the other a meat curry, with rice and vegetables. I priced each one low, at just $5.50 and put the neatly packed meals I'd cooked in a basket to sell door-to-door, with an aim to sell at least 15 each day.

One day, as I went door-to-door, I walked into a business called South Yarra Alterations. The owner, a handsome Greek man named Nick, immediately caught my eye. I asked if he wanted to buy one of my meals, but he surprised me by asking if the kitchen I was cooking from was registered. I had no idea kitchens needed to be registered and when I told him no, he declined, saying he didn't want food poisoning. His comment was a bit mean-spirited, but something about him intrigued me.

Meanwhile, I kept hoping my relationship with Gaz would improve. But nothing changed.

His nightly visits to my apartment, drunk and expecting sex, had lost any feeling of love. I didn't want to give in but it was less painful than being hit.

My mental state was so fragile that the marketing course I'd successfully enrolled in at RMIT, seemed too hard. I only lasted a few months before dropping out and then re-enrolling into a psychology course at Swinburne University. My motivation made sense at the time. I believed the only person who could truly help me was myself. I also believed that studying psychology would help me understand the turmoil in my mind, evaluate the situation and teach me how to deal with things. The ability to regain my own peace of mind was something I craved desperately. Perhaps it would even teach me how to help others who had suffered trauma.

Despite my well-meaning intentions though, after only two semesters, I felt the course was too academic. Instead of focusing on statistics, I wanted to learn about the fundamentals of mental health and develop a deeper human understanding of why people do what they do and what they should do to feel better. The combination of clubbing, babysitting jobs, cooking and selling food for my fledgling business, plus trying to analyse scores of statistics, became too overwhelming.

In the background, my dear friend Jocelyn was urging me to save myself and leave Gaz. No matter how much she begged me to make a change though, I just couldn't do it. There was a part of me that wanted to put an end to the abusive relationship. But the part of me that wanted to save it, was stronger. When I finally realised that I was enough, even though I was nervous about making what I believed was a bold decision, I broke it off with him. I couldn't have known that another monster, my abductor, was about to throw another hurdle in my way.

SECRETS AND LIES

1997-1998

After the court case, I didn't tell anyone Gaz was still visiting me at night. He treated me with such contempt in public, I knew my friends would think I was a fool to still let him have sex with me. I was committed to a relationship that was anything but loving and worthy of loyalty but there were so many emotional strings tying me to him.

Aside from the abuse I had suffered as a child, Gaz was my first and only sexual partner. In my mind, he was essentially my husband. But the bigger, more terrifying truth, was that I was too scared to say no to him. I knew what he was capable of when he was angry.

I did explore seeing other people to help break the hold Gaz had over me. But that only made his jealousy spiral even further out of control. He took to following me at nights to keep tabs on me, sometimes even lurking around my apartment building to see who dropped me home.

The resulting stress made me feel unwell almost all the time, mainly nausea and headaches. I made an appointment with the doctor and, as part of his standard check-up box-ticking, he got me to do a pregnancy test. It was positive. I couldn't believe it.

I was just a kid, only 20. But, despite my fears, the shock very quickly gave way to a feeling of happiness that I couldn't wait to share. When I joined my friends at lunch after the doctor's appointment, I drew in a deep breath and made my announcement.

My friends were disgusted with me. In their eyes, every part of it was wrong. I was too young. Gaz was violent.

They believed I was digging a huge hole that I was about to bury myself and my unborn baby in. But what they didn't understand was, for me, this baby growing inside me wasn't a baby of rape or something conceived of extreme violence. It was my saviour. It would give me a reason to live, to stay alive. By the time I reached home, despite the negative attitudes of my friends, I decided I was going to keep my baby.

That night, I rang another uni friend, Ruwani, who I knew I could trust. She turned out to be the only one who seemed happy for me and genuinely supportive. Next, the biggest hurdle was telling my parents. The shame I had already brought the family was nothing compared to what being a single mother would bring on them. As I'd expected, Mummy also insisted on an abortion.

'No,' I told her. 'I'm keeping this baby.'

I wondered how Gaz would react on learning about the baby. Our baby. A few days later, I went to see him at work and told him I was pregnant.

'No, you're not!' His voice was angry.

'Yes, I am,' I said. 'And I want to keep the baby.'

Gaz looked horrified.

'You mean you want to get married? Are you crazy? How about I take a baseball bat to your stomach?'

My hands slid protectively over my flat belly. I left his workplace quickly, fearing for my life and my baby's. I would have to somehow keep myself and my unborn baby away from Gaz, no matter what.

When I told Ruwani about Gaz's reaction, she insisted I hide at her place for the first few months and, although I desperately wanted to stay in my own cosy apartment, I moved in with Ruwani.

While everyone else around me was telling me I was making a huge mistake, Ruwani focused on the positives of this new life evolving inside me and cared for me like a loving sister, with all the love, attention and nourishment I needed.

When I finally spoke to Daddy, he also made me feel guilty. There he was having an affair with another woman, yet still managing to make me feel guilty about the shame I'd brought on him.

'You're going to give birth to a bastard child, Liza? Your baby has the right to have a father.'

Apart from Ruwani, the only other person who supported my decision, was a midwife at the hospital I presented to for my regular ante-natal check-ups.

'Everything will be okay.' Her belief in me was reassuring. 'I was a single mother once and look at me now. I'm a midwife here. I studied hard and now, here I am. You could stand on your own feet too. Nothing can stop you from having this baby and making something of yourself. There's always a way. You just have to keep going.'

She didn't say much more but seeing how genuinely happy she seemed to be as a single mum inspired me. If she could find a way, so could I.

By the time I came out of hiding, I was too far into the pregnancy for an abortion. When Mummy came to see me, she ordered me to get married.

'You're going to give birth to a bastard child if you don't.'

She then started asking each of Sharul's friends if they would marry me and save me from my shame. One of them said they would, but I refused. I didn't have any feelings for him. I didn't want to marry someone because I was pregnant; I wanted to marry someone I loved.

When Aunty Aish arrived from Malaysia for a visit, her reaction to hearing my "terrible" news was to try and set things right for me. Without my knowledge, she went with Daddy to meet with Gaz's parents and then told me everything had been sorted out. Gaz and I were to be married, but first, we, meaning me and Gaz, would go away on a holiday to discuss the way forward together.

I didn't have a choice in the matter. If I wanted my family in my life, I had to do the right thing and get married. Running away from home years earlier had been a courageous choice, so being pulled back into believing I needed their blessings reinforced those old notions that everything wrong in my life was my fault.

The truth was, I loved my family and I missed them. Maybe if I just shut up and listened to my elders and didn't aggravate Gaz, I'd end up being happily married and also have my family back in my life. Of course, knowing Gaz didn't want to marry me and I didn't want to marry him, were two facts that were hard to ignore.

In my spiritual beliefs though, we're taught to believe everything happens for a reason and everything is already written. For me, this meant my marriage to Gaz and this baby were already written. I knew I had to marry Gaz and set right all that had gone so catastrophically wrong in my life. I'd been a vulnerable kid who was subjected to violence and then ran away to more violence. It was easy to feel my decisions were the cause of my own misery. I decided I would now do only what I was told to by people who seemed to know better than me.

I was desperate to be thought of as someone special by

someone who truly loved me. It broke my heart that the man I was going to marry was cold and aloof. When I became the centre of attention for my relatives and friends in the days leading up to our wedding, I embraced the experience. In that golden moment, I wasn't depressed by memories of the past or worried about the future. I was living in the present, as fleeting as it was, and enjoying the feeling of being cared for.

Everyone, except Gaz, seemed to be eager to help plan the big event. Like most young women facing their wedding day, I wanted to look and feel like a princess. I'd saved as much money as I could and bought myself a cream-coloured dress with a bodice and tight-fitting long sleeves from a wedding shop clearance sale.

No one came with me to watch me try on my dress and I didn't even have my mother by my side to tell me I looked beautiful. Instead, I was all by myself in a bridal wear clearance outlet, trying to buy the best second-hand dress I could for my limited budget. My extended family in Malaysia were coming for the wedding. To go with my $300 gown, I chose some lavender dresses that were on sale from a small boutique at $59.95 each, for the bridesmaids: Jocelyn, Naznina and Snez. Jocelyn felt the dresses were an embarrassment but all three girls kindly helped pay for them.

Gaz didn't want anything too fussy for our wedding. My parents were fine with that; they just wanted to get me married. Even after all the horrible things he'd done to me, I still thought I was lucky to be marrying him.

I let go of so much before walking down that aisle towards him. I'd reached a stage where I believed my wishes didn't matter. What others wanted for me, did. On the wedding day, after giving me the briefest of smiles, he didn't really pay much more attention to me until we had to exchange vows.

When we were asked to repeat the words about being committed to each other 'in sickness and in health,' the silent voice inside my head added, 'and in times of violence and beatings.'

Throughout the nuptials, I kept looking at my family, friends and Mummy, in particular. I was worried if I was doing the right thing and looking for a sign from any one of them that would release me from the decision. I tried hard to stay focused on the wonderful feelings that had buzzed through me when Gaz and I first got involved. I let my mind drift back dreamily to seeing him for the first time in the library and when we went on our first date to McDonalds. None of it was glamorous or especially memorable, but it was all I had. As we worked through a long and dull ceremony, I flipped between feeling scared about what lay ahead for us and telling myself how lucky I was to be marrying the "ideal" husband.

Our wedding reception was held in an English manor house in Ivanhoe. Apart from when we sat together at the head table and made our way around the room to pose for photos and thank our guests, Gaz and I spent most of the time at opposite ends of the room, him with his family and friends and me with mine.

After the reception, my cousins, friends and I changed into saris and went clubbing with Gaz and his friends. When it was time to leave, I cried all the way back to Gaz's house. I knew this was it; my life would never be the same again. I was giving up the safety of my parents' home, where I'd spent the last few wonderful weeks before the wedding, for living with a husband who could be a beast.

We moved my things into his room upstairs at his parents' house. Because both of Gaz's parents had day jobs, it was my responsibility to clean the house every day, a list of duties that included tidying all the rooms, washing the floors and taking care of almost everything required to maintain a household. I even had to scrub the toilets. I felt like Cinderella, but without a fairy godmother to save me.

AMBITIONS AND AWARENESS

1998-2000

Having his own baby growing inside me didn't stop Gaz's assaults on me and, when he threw me down the staircase in his family home and I wet my pants in fear, I thought my waters had broken. My unborn child was still safe but when Gaz's mother's response to her own son's violence was to throw me out of her home, I was forced to postpone my Miss India plans, a business I had been working on to empower women suffering abuse or forced marriages, and moved back to the safety of my parents' home for the last trimester of my pregnancy.

It was the peace, security and serenity I desperately needed and when Aunty Aish came to visit and I was spoiled rotten by my family, my world was perfect again, until my waters did actually break. That's when I found myself in a hospital bed, an ill-informed 21-year-old, having my first child and feeling like I was going out of my mind with the writhing agony of it all. The nurses at my bedside warned me if I didn't push hard enough, there could be complications.

That's when Jocelyn whispered in my ear, 'Liza, we're in this together. When I say push, please push with all the strength you've got, okay? Trust me. Just do as I say.'

I locked eyes with Jocelyn and nodded weakly. Nine hours later, my son arrived, announcing his entry into the world by letting out a mighty yell. Soon afterwards, he was snugly wrapped and placed in my arms. At the sight of his cute, squashed nose and gentle big eyes, all the delivery pain was soon forgotten. I held him close, looked down into his face and whispered to him.

'Hello, King.' And in that moment, I felt like he was there to save me.

Gaz arrived at the hospital 20 minutes after our son was born. I found out later he'd been reluctant to leave the blackjack table at the casino. I chose to focus on the little moments of kindness that kept me going, like when he lifted me from the bed tenderly and carried me to the bathroom to help wash me. I wished I could find a way to draw those moments out of him more often, rather than the bursts of anger I got from him instead. But the fact is, no matter how nice he was in between the anger, it should never have made up for even one cruel comment or assault.

When Mummy and Daddy arrived the next day, I told them I wanted to name my baby Joshua. But when Daddy insisted he be named Adam, pointing out it was the name recognised in Christianity, Judaism and Islam as the first man, I agreed.

Gaz's parents seemed excited to see Adam when they arrived at the hospital the next night but, beyond a few polite words to me, they ignored me completely. Despite their obvious dislike of me, it wasn't long before Daddy began urging me to get back with Gaz and, even when I reminded him of the abuse I'd suffered, it didn't sway his vision of what he thought was best.

'Life isn't about you anymore; it's about the baby,' he said. 'You have to stop being selfish.'

I was torn between doing what our families were saying was the right thing, getting back with Gaz to ensure Adam had a family, and protecting myself. A few weeks later, Gaz and I moved into an apartment in Alphington. Mummy bought all the furniture, set up the nursery and visited us regularly. Having

Adam didn't bring about any change in Gaz's vicious behaviour. To the outside world, we appeared like a normal, middle-class couple. He was a hard-working electrical engineer and project manager. I was the dutiful wife and the two of us had a cute and healthy son we adored.

No one else knew about the pushes, pinches, slaps and hair-pulling that was his reaction to something left lying around the house or if I didn't cook dinner on time. And, although Adam's smile put him in a good mood, it didn't stop him hitting me whenever he was angry, whether Adam was in the room or not. I lost track of how many times the neighbours called the police to investigate our shouts and violent noises but, because I always refused to press charges or admit anything was wrong, no further action was ever taken.

Sometimes, Mummy would have Adam at her place for a sleepover. While Gaz was always happy to do his own thing with his friends, I would welcome the opportunity to feel young and free and head out to a club with Jocelyn. When I was with her, I felt safe and happy. The two of us danced the night away and I felt like I didn't have a care in the world, until it was time to go back to the monster I'd married.

One night, as part of a bigger group of friends at the club, Jocelyn and I agreed to try ecstasy for the first time. Techno music had become something increasingly interesting and intoxicating to me. There was no music or lyrics, but the beat that coursed through my body felt so cleansing. The steady pounding of the bass and drums would take me to a place of euphoria and the drugs enhanced it. In those moments, when my body seemed to become one with the almost primal beat of the music, I could forget the past. Soon, I started going out with my friends every Friday and Saturday night and eventually Sunday nights too.

At home, Gaz would wait up for me for sex. No amount of drugs could prevent the pain his perverse actions inflicted. Worse still, he started filming his assaults on me with a video recorder. I didn't scream or cry out when he abused me, because it would wake Adam and upset him. Instead, I closed my eyes and silently prayed. I wanted to die. But I had to live for my son's sake. I wondered how much more I'd be able to take before I left him for good. Then something happened that finally compelled me to take this decision.

One day, when I was lying face down in bed with Gaz stretched out beside me and Adam still asleep in his cot in the corner of the room, Gaz suddenly jumped on me.

'No Gaz, please…'

He started kissing my neck.

'You are my wife. I've the right to do what I want to.'

I turned my head quickly to the side to look at Adam. I desperately wanted him to stay asleep in his cot.

'Please stop,' I whispered to Gaz.

Gaz ignored my pleas and tried to force himself between my legs. I was pinned to the bed and, as he roughly clamped one of his hands over my mouth, I heard Adam stir in his cot. Gaz finally thrust his way in but, missing his target, ended up raping me from behind instead. Gaz let go of my mouth but continued squeezing my arm tight. By now, Adam was standing in his cot, crying, screaming… and watching.

Adam's vocabulary still hadn't developed much, but that day he found a way to respond to what he was witnessing.

'Dada, stop. Bad Dada. Bad Dada.'

When Gaz finished with me, he got up, showered and left. The physical pain and the horror of seeing the terrified face of my little son, stayed with me long after that. I crawled out of bed, took Adam into my arms and cried.

'Shhh! Mummy's okay.'

But I was far from okay. I realised with sudden clarity that this had gone beyond me. The only way I could protect Adam was by walking away from Gaz. It was something I'd always known, but even just acknowledging it was a huge step.

The next day, when Gaz started belting me again, our neighbour called the police. This time, the police found me bleeding, so they told him to take what stuff he needed and forcefully removed him from our home.

The absence of him in the house for the next seven days gave me strength and time. I found a unit with a courtyard in Ivanhoe. It was an ugly building on the outside, but inside, it was neat and homely. It had two bedrooms and a clean little kitchen. Perfect for Adam and me.

The day I asked Daddy if he would help me with the bond to secure that place, my nervousness was palpable. In the past, he had convinced me to think of my son and to stay with my husband, but now he saw my fear and seemed to understand.

'Yes, Liza.'

I promised I would pay him back.

'Yes, I know,' he said.

When I got home and told Gaz I was leaving, he seemed somewhat subdued, more compliant. I don't know if the police intervention had shaken him up or if he'd been confident I'd never leave him now we had a child together.

The day Adam and I moved to our new home, I'd finally done it. I sat down in my new apartment and cried my heart out. I don't know if they were tears of guilt, of despair, or relief. Perhaps they were a mix of all three.

That night, after my stressful day of setting up my new, safe home for me and my baby, Adam had a sleepover at Mummy's and I went out clubbing with Jocelyn.

Each Saturday night, I worked for the Whiskey Bar to attract more patrons. I'd recruited forty other individuals to bring even more people into the club. By offering the incentives of free entry and drinks to my crew, I achieved the results the club management wanted and my reputation for filling a venue began to spread.

Saying goodbye to Gaz helped me slowly regain my independence and the confidence I'd lost. It wasn't long before I decided to focus on organising a Scream Productions event. Fuelled by my weekend drug dalliances and the false bravado they infused me with, I forged ahead with my first Miss India International show.

I was aware the universities were filled with Indian students, almost all of whom seemed to enjoy attending various Indian events around Melbourne. But those were all small venues that could accommodate only a few hundred people. I wanted to stage a much bigger and grander event, along the lines of well-known international beauty pageants. However, I didn't want mine to include a bikini round. I decided my event would respect the traditions of different cultures and religions and not sexually exploit the women. It was a huge success.

The money I made from this business venture helped me start planning my move to a better apartment and finally buy some decent furniture. When the show I'd helped launch went on to become an annual event, I began to make a name for myself and was even written about in the Indian newspapers in Melbourne. I began to feel like I was unstoppable. It was, however, a short-lived feeling.

HITTING ROCK BOTTOM

2000-2001

It was late afternoon when Gaz turned up at my apartment one day, obviously drunk and banging on the door to be let in. I stood on the other side of the door, begging him to go away. I was scared of what might happen if I did let him enter, but just as scared of what he might do if I didn't. The more Gaz pleaded and pounded at my door, the more I thought it would be better to simply let him in and try to diffuse the situation. But the moment he barged in, he closed the door behind him and started hitting me. Despite his rage, he controlled his blows so none of them landed on my face. Suddenly, he grabbed a knife from the kitchen and tried to shove it into my hand.

'Kill yourself!' he screamed.

From the wild look on his face, his hatred for me was frightening. But for what? Because I left him? Or because I had the courage to finally let him go? When Gaz was in a rage, it always brought on a panic attack in me. I felt breathless and weak.

A part of me wanted to seize that knife, take my life and put an end to it all. All the pain, physical, mental and emotional, would be finally over. But it would also mean Adam being left without the love and protection of a mother. If it wasn't for Adam, I would've perhaps killed myself that day. I had to use every dreg of will-power to fight the urge.

When I didn't take the knife, Gaz threw me across the room.

My body slammed into a pane of panelled glass, shattering pieces all around me as I fell into a heap on the ground. The shock of his sudden arrival and the assault, brought on a full-blown panic attack and my hysterical screams were so loud that Gaz called Jocelyn to control me.

She and her sister, Marilyn, rushed to my house to find me wailing on the floor.

'Liza, you're safe now. I'm here. Everything is going to be okay.'

Jocelyn rocked me against her body and wiped my tears as Marilyn swept up the glass. Gaz was nowhere to be seen. As I quietened down, Jocelyn encouraged me to see a solicitor to apply for full custody of Adam. I knew she was right.

Considering Gaz's violence and the fact that I was single-handedly looking after Adam, I thought it might be easy. On paper, however, Gaz came out looking like the more suitable parent. He had a career as an engineer and his parents were well-respected and had high-paying jobs. I was just a single mother who seemed to have an endless stream of bad things happen to me.

When the case eventually came up, the court awarded us shared custody, with more time allocated to me, to maintain the regularity of Adam's life as much as possible, while still enabling him to form a relationship with his father. Gaz had him from Thursday night until Monday morning every second weekend. Those four nights were more painful and lonely than I can put into words.

At first, to escape the stress of being separated from Adam, I started taking ecstasy more often. But I quickly moved on to taking harder drugs. I started taking speed to increase the high of the ecstasy tablet and cocaine, when I could afford it, to make me feel like a rock star while out clubbing. Many of the new friends

I made in the club scene were drug dealers and so I hardly ever had to pay for drugs. My close friends didn't like giving them to me, but I needed them to forget my anguish, to numb my brain. Before I knew it, on the weekends Gaz had Adam, my partying began on Thursday nights as soon as my son left to be with him. I felt helpless each time I couldn't stop Adam being taken away from me. Getting out of it was a way to control something in my life and lose control all at the same time. Anything to dull my longing for my son.

On Friday nights, my friends and I would hit the club, where I would typically take up to three ecstasy tablets, as well as snorting speed. I'd return home on Saturday mornings around eleven, when most people are hitting the gym, or doing their food shopping, and either take sleeping tablets to help me sleep or smoke a joint to calm my nerves.

On Saturday nights, I had to start work by 9.30 pm at the Whiskey Bar, where I managed the whole of level three as the club's main promoter. But neither the sleeping tablets nor the use of drugs would help me sleep. I'd lie down on my bed, my eyes shut tight, my mind wandering, thinking about everything in my life: the past, the present, the music, the drugs, everything. By the time I eventually fell asleep, it would usually be around 7 pm and I'd get up less than two hours later. The only thing that could keep me going for another night was to do it all again and take more drugs.

By the time Adam was dropped back to me Monday morning, my poor body had endured the wear and tear of spending the last four days on a high and dancing non-stop without any nutritious food to fuel it. Not only would my insides ache from hunger, but my mouth was aching with the blisters that came from my drug-induced habit of chewing gum for days and biting the inside of my lips and cheeks without being aware of doing it. Many people tried to warn me that drugs were bad, drugs would kill me. I was convinced they were wrong. I felt so confident, so strong, invincible!

Gaz and I were no longer a couple but as co-parents, the toxicity between us continued and life became an endless cycle of court cases in my attempt to get more custody of Adam. My mother sat patiently by my side through every appearance and that support meant so much to me. Her interest in the custody arrangements was about more than me, though.

Despite our previous periods of difficulty and occasional estrangements, my mother and father were back in my life as Adam's hands-on grandparents and, because they spent every second weekend with Adam on the weekend he was not with Gaz, I was free to keep on partying each weekend. My own bond with them was still in tatters but, for me, it was important for my son to have that relationship. Knowing they loved having him, made it easier for me to ignore the fact I had a drug problem.

Before Adam came home to me at the end of each weekend, I cleaned the house and cooked food I could feed him, ignoring the exhaustion that was killing me and trying to be the best mother I could be. In my heart though, I knew he deserved a much better mother than one who seemed to be constantly making wrong choices.

By the time Adam was two years old, Gaz had a new girlfriend. Her name was Chelsea. One Sunday, Adam was to be delivered to my place by 6 pm. But when it was time for his arrival, I was still feeling drug-affected and, with the combination of partying, fatigue, lack of food and the physical labour of cleaning the house, I fell into a deep sleep until the sound of Gaz's parents knocking on the door woke me.

We exchanged brief pleasantries and then they handed Adam to me. He came willingly enough to me, but I noticed he never took his eyes off Gaz's folks. He'd clearly enjoyed being with them and seemed to be struggling to let them go, despite being back home with me.

Once they left, I hugged and kissed Adam again and again. I set him down on my bed and tickled him until he started giggling. I warmed his milk and lay on the bed with him. I was desperate for sleep, but Adam was wide awake. He crawled backwards off the bed. When he refused to be coaxed into coming back to me, I got out of bed and sat on the floor with him.

'What's wrong, Adam?'

'I want Chelsea. Chelsea Mumma.'

His reply stunned me.

'What did you say?' I yelled at him.

'Chelsea Mumma, Chelsea Mumma,' he said over and over again.

'She's not your Mumma!' I screamed at him.

I could feel the rage surging up through my chest and constricting my throat. I raised my hand and brought it down with a smack on his bottom. He gasped and started screaming.

I screamed even louder, 'She's not your Mumma! I am!'

A horrible resentment swirled inside me. Here I was, fighting Gaz over him, but Adam wanted to be with them, with Gaz, who'd wanted to hit me on the stomach with a baseball bat and his parents who turned a blind eye to their son's violence against me. I grabbed Adam and hugged him. He was still crying. I couldn't believe what I'd just done to the most important person in my life.

'Baby, Mummy loves you. I'm so sorry. I'm so, so sorry,' I cried repeatedly, hugging him to my chest.

The shock of losing control with my child like that should have been enough of a reason to stop taking drugs anymore, but I felt helpless without them. My friend, Natalie, was disgusted with the way I was sinking deeper into drug addiction and had started keeping her distance from me. She threatened to call child protection because she felt sorry for Adam. I wasn't beating him or leaving him home alone, but I wasn't looking after him properly either. She wanted it to be a wake-up call for me, but how could I change my mindset when the drugs were muddling it even more?

Eventually, the drugs no longer helped numb my pain and my recurring bouts of depression became harder to kick. I asked Snez, now my brother's ex-wife, to move into a house in Preston with me. I told her it was hard being a single mum and that I'd feel better if I had someone with me and if Gaz knew I didn't live alone.

Snez had always been loving and caring towards me, like a sister figure. I knew these feelings wouldn't stop just because she was no longer with Sharul. I was immensely relieved when she agreed.

One weekend, after we'd partied harder than usual, Jocelyn dropped me home at around 9 am. The moment she left to go back to her own place, a feeling of being deserted came over me. I felt utterly alone. My thoughts turned to Adam. I was convinced he didn't need me. He would be much better off if he didn't have me in his life. I felt utterly worthless. My life meant nothing. I was nothing.

I dropped some ecstasy tester into a glass of lemonade and sculled it. Flashes of my life: rape, family violence, kidnap, the bitterness, loneliness, isolation, raced through my head. The glass dropped from my hand and I collapsed on the floor. Foam began frothing out of my mouth and my body started convulsing.

When Snez found me, a moment later, she screamed and called an ambulance.

The next instant, by some coincidence, or perhaps because of a mother's intuition that her child needed help, Mummy called me on my mobile. Snez quickly took the call, and blurted out what had happened, adding that an ambulance from the nearby Austin Hospital would arrive any minute. As the doctors started attaching things to my body, I kept pleading with them, struggling to get the words out of my mouth. 'Adam … my son, Adam … please don't take him away from me.'

It was as if I was having an out-of-body experience. It felt as if I'd been lifted somewhere high up and was looking down at the swarm of doctors around my limp body. Suddenly, I was conscious of being on my back on a hospital bed and a female nurse peering into my face.

'You're an angel,' she said, smiling. 'No one's going to take your son. You're an angel.'

For a moment, I thought, Am I now really an angel? Or is that lady just feeling sorry for me and only trying to make me feel better?

I survived yet another suicide attempt and left the hospital as soon as I could. All I wanted to do was get home and be with my precious little son, Adam. Things had to change and I was the only one who could change them.

So, when Sharul spilled the beans on problems he was grappling with at work and asked if I could help him, what followed turned out to be the opportunity I needed to finally escape.

TURNING THE CORNER

2002

I didn't see my brother Sharul very often, but I was always happy when we did connect in person. He focused on his life, I focused on mine, but even if we did only catch up every month or two, I always considered him my best friend. When he called and asked me to meet him at a café in the city the next afternoon, I arrived at a funky, dark, underground-type venue, Piccolo Café, and happily accepted his offer to buy me a soft drink.

'So, what do you think of my café?'

His café? His question surprised me. It made me feel incredibly proud of him and it was great knowing I had a place to chill out whenever I felt like it. Over the next few months, I became a regular visitor to his Piccolo Café and getting the odd free drink definitely helped my tight budget.

But one morning, around 10.30 am, I turned up to find the doors locked and the cafe in darkness. I could see him through the glass, sleeping inside, so I banged on the doors until he woke up and let me in.

The café was a mess from the previous day's trading and his rumpled look told me he'd slept in his clothes from the day before. On closer inspection, the fridges were half empty and the whole place was filthy. Had he been trying to manage on his own without any staff? Perhaps he wasn't making enough money any longer. After quizzing him about his situation, he confessed that it wasn't the first time he'd slept in the café and he often kept it closed. How did he go from successful café owner to this sad state so quickly?

'What's going on, Anne?' I asked, using the respectful South Indian term for brother that we always used in Malaysia. It was how I'd been brought up to address him.

He sat down and sighed, 'I'm having a hard time keeping the café going.'

I knew how much he loved to party and, in addition to trying to run the cafe on his own, with little financial back-up and no emotional or physical support from staff, his situation had driven him to exhausted burn-out. What he said next stunned me into silence.

'Noli,' he said (he always called me that), 'you're going through some rough times. I know that. I'm sorry I haven't been a good brother. Now, I want to do something for you and for Adam. I want to give you something to help you make a life for yourself and him. I want to give you this café.'

I opened my mouth to say something, but words failed me.

'No, don't say anything,' Sharul said. 'This place is dead. But it isn't a complete failure. I want to give it to you. If there's anyone who could turn things around here, it's you. I am sure of that.'

How could I accept this offer? I didn't know the first thing about managing a café, let alone one that was already on the back foot and running at a loss. I had some experience, on a basic level, of preparing and selling a couple of food items door to door to a small group of people. But that was as far as my knowledge of the hospitality industry went. How would I prepare a whole menu of food and beverages for a larger crowd of diverse customers? How would I staff the café? I was afraid of biting off more than I could chew, but I also understood that my brother seemed to have hit a roadblock in his business and was struggling to keep going. He obviously needed support. As we talked more, I learned he was on the verge of losing the café completely. I felt an obligation to support Sharul and make his idea work, especially since he had thought so lovingly of Adam and me.

Suddenly, I felt a rush of joy roaring through my head. Oh my God! I thought. I was going to have a café of my own in the city! The exciting possibilities the venture offered, flashed before my eyes. I wouldn't be a fool and mess things up now. I'd clean the place and do whatever I could to make it the best one in the laneway, if not in the entire neighbourhood. I'd cook the best meals, serve the best coffees. But then reality interrupted my daydreams. Melbournians loved their coffee and I had no clue how to brew one. Plus, I had no spare savings to invest in getting the equipment I'd need. From floating on air, I crash-landed back to earth.

Sharul held out the key to me. I looked around the café that once looked like a groovy hangout, the place to be. It now looked like a cheerless little dungeon. A lot needed to be fixed. It seemed hopeless but a ray of light shone through those dark thoughts and inspired me. I'd change things, give it my unique touch, tweak it to my style, make it my kind of place. I didn't know how. Just that I would.

I looked at Sharul's outstretched hand and took the key to the Piccolo Café. He was in a terrible situation, but more importantly, he was my brother and I loved him. This had to work and I would make sure of it.

I turned up to work the very next day.

Sharul had told me he needed a couple of months to sort himself out but, having nobody there to guide me, turned out to be a gift. As I sat at a table inside Sharul's deserted café, I thought about all the things I didn't know and needed to learn: leases, landlords, stocking up on provisions, promoting the café, dealing with neighbouring cafés. The list went on and on. Next, I took a deep breath and thought about what I did know. I knew how to answer the phone. I knew how to talk to people and put them at ease. And I knew stuff about the music industry and a little about promoting a business.

It seemed like a beginning, at least, so I ran from there. I thought about the music I'd play in the café and shortlisted my choices. I called all my friends to help out and together, we painted the walls in bright, attention-grabbing colours – red, green, pink and orange.

We set a few tables and chairs outside in the alley with umbrellas and I bought cheerful-looking geraniums from a local florist. As patrons entered the alley and approached the café, they were greeted by flowers on each table, the sounds of French house music and the mouth-watering aromas of some of my favourite Indian dishes. The crowds started coming in.

Satisfying the food tastes of lawyers, uni students, police personnel and a variety of business people, was intimidating at first. I was still trying to get my head around things like safe food handling practices, rent payments and offering an interesting variety of coffees and a more diverse menu. But I must've been doing something right, because we were soon catering to a full house every day.

About six weeks after revamping the café, the feeling that I'd been given another chance in life, after surviving my suicide attempt and having Sharul offer me the café, was overwhelming. I was grateful but also determined to work hard and create my own destiny. This opportunity was too important to waste.

Even my parents became regular visitors. Daddy caught the

train into the city and, when he walked into the bustling Piccolo Café the first time one afternoon, he had a big smile on his face. But as soon as he spotted me, he said, 'Where's Adam?'

'Do you like the café?' I asked him.

'Yes, it's very nice, Liza. But where is Adam?'

'Are you proud of me, Daddy?'

'Of course, I'm proud of you, Liza. How could I not be? But tell me, where's Adam? I want to see Adam.'

I kept Adam at a crèche while I was at work. So, we went there and picked him up and Daddy took him home on the train to my home in Mill Park. I knew it would be a great bonding opportunity for them and could see how thrilled my little son was. But I was left still searching for that approval that put me at the centre of my father's thoughts for once. I just wanted him to recognise my efforts and my evolution.

It was a similar story with Mummy. Whenever she stopped by, she never stayed long because of the limited parking time and her fear of getting a parking ticket. In the time that she was there, she'd offer to cook for me and ask me what I needed help with but, because I knew she was always in such a rush, I never accepted. Her visits would usually involve her hurrying in to deliver a freshly baked cake and quickly leaving again.

She was clearly supporting me by baking for the café. But I was also hungry for more from her and simply wanted her to take the time to be in the moment with me, to enjoy the mother-daughter times I felt I'd missed for most of my life and to hear her utter the words of approval and love that my heart ached for.

I still partied on weekends. But being so busy with the café during the week had reduced my drug use significantly and I was healthier and happier. On the weekends, when my friends gathered at the cafe as the launchpad to yet another night of taking ecstasy and dancing the night into daytime, I still had fun in those drug-fuelled moments but spent more time thinking about how I could finally move away from the world of nightclubs and drugs permanently.

My last suicide attempt had scared me and I was afraid of the paranoia these drugs caused. I didn't want anything to give in to my darker thoughts and have something bad happen to me, not when the prospects of Adam and me having a better life were so much brighter now. Now I had a reason to stay clean. I had a purpose in life. My determination to make the café a huge success had seen me build a strong and consistent patronage for the business. There was finally a light at the end of what had been such a long and dark tunnel.

Customers genuinely enjoyed chatting with me and those who knew I was a single mum told me what a great job I was doing with the café while raising a child on my own, though they had no clue about how long my days really were. Their positive opinions of me went a long way toward boosting my confidence and my belief in myself.

Each weekday started at 6 am when I'd wake up, get ready and then take Adam on the train with me to buy that day's food for the café. I'd get off a few stops later with Adam in the pram, go straight to the market to buy fresh produce, then get back on the train to go to the café, where I would set up things and wait for my assistant to come. After dropping Adam at crèche, I'd return to the café, open up and start trading. With only one girl helping me, it was non-stop work all day. At three, I would pick Adam up from crèche, and keep him with me at the café until we finished at seven and closed for the night.

At the end of each day, we returned home with a wad of cash. I rarely got time to go deposit it in the bank, so I paid my rent and suppliers with cash and kept the rest in a wallet under my bed. I didn't know about taxes, let alone that I had to pay them. As exhausting as my day was, it was a great feeling knowing I'd turned a loss-making business into a popular hangout, single-handedly.

Running the café made me feel so much stronger. I was no longer just a single parent; I was a successful small business owner.

Gaz and I would always be connected as Adam's parents, of course, but I was finally ready to cut every other possible tie I could. I had to get a divorce. Walking up the stairs toward the Women's Legal Service sign, I thought about all the different ways women in need were supported in Australia: help lines, pregnancy lines, women's legal support. It was simply fantastic. The lawyer I saw that day explained that since Gaz and I had moved back in together for a brief period during the time we were estranged, our separation time would be considered too short for an immediate divorce. But we could still try to get one because of the violence that had plagued our union.

Months later, when we had our first day in family court, it turned out that being granted a divorce right away was too much to expect. When my lawyer declared that we were filing for divorce after seven months of separation, Gaz's response was to state he didn't want a divorce. He told the judge he wanted to make the marriage work and needed more time for this. On top of that, he claimed the papers hadn't been served on him properly. The case was adjourned to a later date and I left the court feeling terribly depressed. How could the court let him still control my life like that when I wanted to start afresh and put the pain, he had caused me, behind me?

After that, each time he was served court papers at his office, he didn't accept them. And when my lawyer got the clerk to serve him at his parents' house, his parents wouldn't accept the papers either. We finally got a court date a few months later. Gaz turned up looking handsome in carefully pressed clothes, briefcase in hand, clearly determined to create a good impression as the "good guy" perfect husband. When Gaz's lawyer and I exchanged glances, I noticed the smug expression on his face. You're an arsehole, defending a monster, I thought. How the hell can you even live with yourself?

The judge confirmed there was a separation of at least twelve months and asked me if I really wanted a divorce.

'Yes,' I began, 'because he has been excessively abusive, he's mean, he beats me up like—'

The judge abruptly held up his hand. 'I'm sorry, you've been through that part already. But this hearing isn't about that. Have you charged him for the crimes against you?'

'No, I haven't.'

'Well, you have to go through the proper procedures to charge him for things like that. This court hearing is only about the divorce. Do you want it?'

I wanted to plead with the judge to listen to me. Don't you care? I'm telling you what a hell my life has been. I don't have the energy to go through any more procedures. My abusive husband and I are here in court right now. You're a judge. Can't you handle it all now and charge him? But of course, I knew the system didn't work like that, so I said only what I was directed to.

'Yes, I want a divorce.'

Then it was Gaz's turn.

'I don't want a divorce, but I will agree to it if that's what she really wants.'

The judge granted the divorce. As we walked out of the courtroom, I looked at Gaz.

'Bye, Liza,' he said.
'Bye, Gaz.'

And that was it. I walked away feeling excited. And so free. I tried to do that little skip people do, jumping and clicking their feet together in the air. But I wasn't very good at it. Still, my life felt more uncomplicated than it had felt in years. Jocelyn and I went out to celebrate and my head buzzed with the possibility of a safe and wonderful future. A future that I could control.

PART TWO

REGAINING CONTROL

A NEW BEGINNING

2002–2004

Co-parenting, when there is such a challenging history, is difficult. But it is possible. Now that I had turned the Piccolo Café into a thriving business, I had something I needed to prove to myself more than to Gaz, really. I wasn't scared anymore. I had achieved something meaningful and successful. I was capable. I am a survivor. When I called Gaz to pick up Adam for his weekend, I directed him to drive down Flinders Lane and park near the side of the cafe. I was feeling particularly confident that day. I'd just dyed my hair a caramel colour and got a new hairstyle with a fringe. Those little cosmetic things often gave me a boost and, as shallow as it might seem, they did wonders for my self-esteem.

I held Adam's hand as we stepped out of the café and walked up the alleyway to Gaz's green BMW. As I put him into his seat, I said, 'Enjoy your time with Daddy. Give Mummy a kiss.'

Adam hugged and kissed me, and as I stepped back from the car, Gaz said, 'So, this is where you work?'

'No, this is my café. I own it.'

'Really?' Gaz said, raising an eyebrow and looking toward the café. 'When did this happen?'

'It happened,' I said calmly. I didn't owe him any explanations. 'Would you like to step in? Have a drink, a coffee, maybe?'

'No, it's okay.'

I could see how shocked he was. 'Are you all right, Gaz?'

'Yes, of course. But the café looks good. Congratulations, Liza.'

The look on Gaz's face seemed to change from shock to pride as he looked back at me. It looked like I'd just jumped at least 10 notches higher in his eyes.

'Sure you don't want to come in?' I said.

'No, I have to go.'

There was something in his eyes. Regret? It was the first time I seemed to be the one who had the power in our relationship. After that, whenever he picked Adam up each fortnight, I noticed Gaz looked at me differently. Perhaps he was confused about how well I was doing after our divorce. He had obviously expected me to crumble and the fact I had become stronger, must have gnawed at him and his mistaken perceptions.

When the time was right, I knew I wanted someone who saw me for who I really was.

I didn't realise that time would come so soon.

One day, while I was out getting groceries for the café, I bought a new dress that was a bit too loose for me. As I stepped off the tram, wondering where to get it altered, I spotted a man approaching and realised it was Nick, the tailor from South Yarra Alterations. I remembered him from when I had tried to sell him one of my meal packages. Back then, he had asked if my kitchen was registered and when I said no, he had declined to buy my food, citing concerns about food poisoning. It felt like a twist of fate that the very person I needed was right there when I'd just been thinking about having my dress adjusted.

As Nick and I continued walking toward each other on the footpath, I lost my grip on my grocery bags. He bent down and helped me pick them up as he recognised me. As we stood up, he kissed me on the cheek. I knew that kiss was just a friendly greeting, but I felt something stir inside me. He wasn't the kind of guy I was looking for. I remembered how Mummy had once joked that when I found the guy for me, he would be bald, chubby and wearing glasses. And now, in front of me stood Nick: bald, a little chubby and wearing glasses. I didn't understand why seeing him was giving me that flutter, but it certainly felt good being this close to him.

We exchanged polite pleasantries and I told him about the café and he told me he didn't usually come into the city and was only there on an errand. An awkward silence arose. I knew I wanted to talk some more with him.

'Would you like to visit the café?' I blurted. There was a battle of some kind going on inside me. He wasn't my type at all, yet something drew me to him. Was it the suave businessman he was or the strong feeling we'd been brought together for a reason? I couldn't say for sure.

'That would be nice,' Nick said.

As we sat at a side table at Piccolo's and sipped beer, he told me about the newsagency he was in the process of opening up.

Suddenly, I said, 'Do you want to go on a date with me?'

He was taking a sip of beer at the time and nearly choked on it.

'Excuse me?'

So, I asked him again, feeling a little less sure of myself after his initial reaction.

'Yes!' he said, this time with a wide, bright smile on his face that seemed to light up the entire café.

For our first date, we went to a Greek restaurant – Remvi by the Bay. It was empty, but in a romantic sort of way, as if he'd requested it. All the staff seemed to know Nick and were very attentive. We didn't have to order. Platters of food: dips, calamari, fish, and meats, were whisked to our table and placed in front of us.

We chatted easily as we ate.

'Where did you go?' Nick said. 'You were living on Clara Street and then you just disappeared.'

I told him about the kidnapping and he was shocked. He hadn't heard about it. Then I told him about Gaz and Adam.

'So sorry to hear this,' he said. 'I'd gone to your apartment to look for you a few times. But I never saw you again until I bumped into you in the club that time I made that stupid joke about you coming back to my place for a threesome with my girlfriend. I was so happy to see you again.'

I was being wined and dined in a way I'd never been before and I could tell he really enjoyed my company. Even when he told me he'd gone back to the nightclub a number of times to try and meet me again, I wasn't alarmed and I didn't think he'd been stalking me. Rather, I loved the way he made me feel safe and cared for and I loved the kind look of genuine interest on his face as he listened to me. He was being romantic and a thorough gentleman.

The more we talked, the more I knew I could easily fall in love with him. But Adam was never far from my mind. So finally, I decided to come clean with Nick. I told him, in my opinion, this relationship we both seemed interested in pursuing just wouldn't work. I was a single parent, which meant he would have to consider being a father to Adam as an integral part of our association with each other. Adam, in turn, would need to get used to looking at him as a father figure. And considering our diverse spiritual backgrounds, I adhered to certain beliefs. If he wanted to marry me, it would have to be a ceremony aligned with those principles.

Nick listened quietly as I continued to outline all the reasons a relationship between us wouldn't work.

'I'm not saying I want to get married now,' I continued. 'I've just got out of a bad marriage and I certainly don't want to go through another bad one. But then again, I'm not looking for some fun fling either. Which is why I want someone who wants a more permanent relationship, a more serious commitment.'

I was pretty sure most guys would've run a mile by this point. But Nick waited for me to finish and simply said, 'I'd like to see where this goes.'

He said he'd been in a relationship with a female bisexual, an open relationship where they were free to date others, but soon realised that wasn't how he wanted to live the rest of his life.

'As for Adam,' he said, 'don't worry. I won't see your son just yet, but when I do, he can call me Baba.'

I later found out from a friend that Baba was Greek for Dad. It was a great first date. I was relieved to have been able to talk freely about my concerns and I felt even better knowing Nick understood them.

He drove me home and walked me to my door. I could feel the heat between us as he leaned toward me and kissed me on the cheek again. He smelled nice and I thought to myself that he wasn't bad looking either. Moreover, he didn't make a move on me and I thought that added to the wonderfully sweet impression he'd made on me.

The next morning there was a knock on the door, and I found a locksmith from South Yarra on my doorstep.

'Nick sent me to change the locks on your house,' he said.

I called Nick and asked him what was going on. The last thing I wanted was to be going out with a psycho or a control freak like Gaz.

'I want you to be safe,' he said, calmly. 'I don't want anyone getting in the house and hurting you.'

His concern was touching. On our next date, we went to see a movie at Northland and, once again, he was the perfect gentleman. I couldn't help thinking there had to be something wrong with the guy. He seemed too good to be true. When we got home that day, we had coffee and sat on the floor and watched TV together. And again, he didn't make a move on me. Until that day, he had only kissed me on the cheek. On an impulse, I made the first serious move and put my lips to his.

From there, it moved quickly, a rush in intimacy that we clearly both wanted and needed. It didn't feel like our second date because we'd known each other over such a long time. But while there were no embarrassing moments when we got intimate, it didn't feel that special either. Intimacy was something I still seemed to be struggling with.

The following weekend, I went to a rave with Jocelyn. But something inside me had already shifted. I didn't dance all night as usual. I didn't drink either. Instead, I spent the entire night, from eleven at night to seven in the morning, sitting on a couch, texting with Nick.

It was the first time Jocelyn and I had been out in a few weeks, and I could see she was annoyed by my behaviour.

The following week, Nick and I were supposed to go out together. But we never made it out the door. We didn't merely have sex that night. We made love. For the first time in my life, it felt wonderful to be intimate with someone. It felt so right. He held me in his arms all night and when the sunlight woke me up the next morning, I felt rested and at peace. The bed felt comfortable, there were birds chirping outside and Nick was still holding me. I felt like I'd finally come home.

I sat on Nick's lap as we ate breakfast and cuddled. It seemed so easy and natural to trust him. There was no denying it; despite initially doubting my feelings for him, the truth was, I was falling in love with him… fast. The feeling left me uneasy. After breakfast, he had his own revelation to share with me.

'There's something I need to tell you, Liza. I understand you might have never experienced what it's like to be really happy, to be treated well, to be loved and so, you might wonder whether what I feel for you is the real thing. But the truth is, I love what we have. And I'd better make this clear—I'm here to stay.'

I was amazed by his perceptiveness. I hadn't realised I was subconsciously thinking of ending our relationship just because it was so wonderful and good, but he was right. This was the kind of relationship I'd never had before. In my mind, despite the growth I'd achieved, I still had this niggling feeling I didn't deserve it. I thought about all the good relationships I'd sabotaged and the bad ones I'd hung on to. I just gazed back at Nick in silence, wondering if he already knew me better than I knew myself.

I continued to listen to Nick, not saying a word, as he suggested I needed counselling and the right support to help me adjust into a healthy and happy relationship for the first time, adding he would always be there by my side, come what may.

I didn't doubt that I needed counselling. But in the past, I'd always believed I needed it to help me deal with a troubled relationship and an abusive husband. I never thought it could help me accept love from a good man. It would still be a while though, a few years actually, before I explored taking the counselling route as the way forward.

Two weeks later, we decided it was time for Nick to meet Adam. When he came over and knocked on the door, Adam opened it.

'Hi, I'm Baba,' Nick said.

'Hi, Baba,' Adam replied.

Nick seemed to have no problem making friends with Adam and even began playing a few games with him and me. The three of us were relaxed and enjoying our time together. Suddenly, there was a knock on the door. Aunty Aish, who was in Melbourne visiting at that time, had decided to drop in unannounced. The moment I realised Aunty Aish and Uncle Hamd were at the door, I quickly asked Nick to hide and both of us raced upstairs. I hid him in my bedroom cupboard, rushed back downstairs and opened the door. The first thing Uncle Hamd did as he walked in the door was point at Nick's shoes and ask Adam, 'Whose shoes are those?'

'Baba's,' Adam said, his attention on the toy car in his hand. 'He's upstairs in the bedroom cupboard.'

Aunty Aish and Uncle Hamd looked at me, clearly shocked. 'What?' they said simultaneously.

'No, no, what on earth are you talking about, Adam?' I said, shaking my head and trying to pass it off as the silly comment of a confused four-year-old and casually changed the subject. My aunt and uncle didn't stay long, but off and on they kept looking at me suspiciously. After they left, I breathed a huge sigh of relief. I went upstairs and found Nick fast asleep on my bed.

A week or so later, I was having coffee with Daddy at Piccolo's when Nick arrived. I'd told Nick a little about Daddy and when I introduced the two of them to each other, Nick said to him, 'Just a sec. I've got something for you.'

He ran back to his car and surprised both Daddy and me by returning with a Yanni CD, Daddy's favourite music. The guy always seemed to be doing all the right things.

The very next day, Nick and I were supposed to be going

out on a date. We drove off in his car and, a short while later, he slowed down.

'I have to stop and see someone first,' he said.

We pulled up outside a suburban house. He wanted me to meet his aunty, he said. Oh, this must be a favourite aunt, I thought. Then he took me to his cousin's house. What I didn't know was, the next person I'd be meeting would be the most important person in his life – his mother.

I remembered his mum from when I'd first visited his tailoring shop. I was nervous about meeting her because on that last occasion, when I'd interacted with her as a customer, she'd come across as cold and aloof.

Now, as we surprised her with our arrival, she let us into her house in her pyjamas with a terse hello and not even a hint of a smile on her face. She clearly had no interest in meeting me.

A week later, Nick and I took Adam to try again and have yum cha with her. Her unrelenting silence made it obvious she didn't want to be there with us. Then, she spoke to Nick in Greek. He later told me, she had asked him how long "this" would go on. She wanted him to stop seeing someone like me, someone who was a single parent.

Despite his mother's obvious dislike of our relationship, Nick and I continued to see each other and whenever Adam was with Gaz, I stayed at Nick's place. I tried to make sure Nick's mother's behaviour toward me didn't get me down. The important thing was that Nick and I were together and he and Adam got along like buddies. Nick, himself, continued to show me time and again how supportive he was of me. Life was lovely.

Then, out of the blue, my peace of mind was shattered in a way I hadn't imagined. I received a phone call telling me Mummy was very ill and in the Royal Women's Hospital. I got to the hospital just as she was being wheeled into an operating theatre. She'd been diagnosed with ovarian cancer.

Daddy had worked with cancer patients every day, but I'd never really understood what it was all about. That seemed like another world. Now, cancer was in my world, inside my mother.

I couldn't stop crying when the doctor explained her condition to me. The doctor explained the surgery had gone well but that piece of positive news didn't register with me. Nothing got through to my brain except the fact my mother had cancer.

It took Mummy getting cancer for me to realise how much I truly loved her. I was absolutely distraught. Just the thought that I could lose her was unbearable. I now found I had all the room in my heart to forgive her for not standing up for me in the past. I accepted that mothers can make mistakes. I knew I had made plenty of my own mistakes with Adam. If I had been a great mummy, I wouldn't have taken drugs or even been involved in that dangerous scene after I had a child.

I was in the middle of organising another Miss India International show and Asia expo when I'd received that devastating phone call about my mother's illness. I'd already booked and paid the deposit for the Melbourne Convention Centre for the event and started taking bookings for the expo's 300 exhibitor spaces. I was hoping for a sell-out event for Miss India that year, which was to be launched during the expo. I was a flourishing entrepreneur with big dreams, but now, even after selling a good number of exhibitor spaces, I felt as if I didn't have the strength in me to go ahead with both events. All I wanted was to be by Mummy's side. There was no way I could hold a major event and still be there for her. I cancelled the expo without a second thought. I would lose a lot of money, but I didn't care. I didn't want to lose Mummy.

My world became her treatment schedule. I went to all her chemotherapy and radiation appointments. I felt so helpless witnessing the effects of the cancer treatment. The vomiting, the intolerable pain, her hair falling out in clumps.

Nick never wavered in his support of me through it all. He seemed to know exactly what to do, when to leave me be and when to be there. When Sharul turned up at the café one afternoon and confronted me with an outrageous decision, Nick's support became more invaluable than ever.

'We need to talk, Noli,' he said, sitting down at one of the tables, looking fresh and sharp, dressed in a stylish jacket and golfing cap. 'You've done a great job with the café. But I'm sorry, I'm going to have to take it over again, take it back from you.'

I couldn't believe what he'd just said.

'What do you mean you're going to have to take over the café? This is my café! You gave it to me, remember? You said you had nothing else to give me and that was why you were going to give me this place!'

'But I paid for it and still owe money on it,' he replied.

I was furious.

'If I hadn't taken over and turned things around, you would've lost it anyway. Now that things look good, you want to take it back? Look around you; I did all this! I brought customers back here. You take over this café and you're going to make a mess of everything again. All my hard work will go down the drain. I'm telling you, that's what will happen for sure.'

'No, Noli. This is what I need to do. And I'm going to do it.'

I left the café, stunned and feeling lost. Sharul didn't even give me an opportunity to be his partner. My own brother had used me and now he was casting me aside. That café had made me financially independent, given me my freedom, made me the confident person I was. Plus, for me as a single mother, losing it meant a risk of losing Adam too. My image of being a financially sound mother in the eyes of the court would take a beating. What if Gaz took me to court again?

As I walked along Collins Street, I gazed into the boutiques and glanced at the dresses on display without actually seeing them. I was trying hard to focus on something positive in my life at that moment – my relationship with Nick. I'd already started getting involved in his alterations business and had begun picking up a few new accounts for his shop. Perhaps I was destined to work for Nick, I thought.

I stopped walking and called him. He was upset to hear what I told him. He'd been making plans to open a creperie store nearby so I could sell crepes at the café, but now his main concern was for me.

'Are you going to sell it to him? You raised the value of that café.'

'No, I'm walking away. I can start again,' I told Nick. But I was also telling myself the same thing. After a brief pause, I said, 'Could I work with you and help build accounts?'

He didn't hesitate to answer.

'Of course you can.'

Nick's assertion wasn't surprising. Just wonderfully reassuring. I wasn't that confident about entering an industry I still knew so little about, but I'd done that before and knew I could do it again.

When Sharul was all set to resume managing the café again, the landlord said Sharul could settle his debts by paying him a lump sum. They could call it even and he would let him continue in the café. Despite how I felt about Sharul abruptly taking the café back from me, I asked Nick to loan Sharul some money toward the payment of the lump sum. I might not have been running the café anymore, but it had played such a significant role in restoring my confidence in myself and my abilities, that I didn't want to see it gone.

However, the café never ran as well again under Sharul's management and, in the end, he lost it because the landlord refused to renew his lease. Ironically, a creperie business took over the site.

Nick and I were working well together, both personally and professionally, but I was still partying with my friends and he wasn't happy about my drug taking. He never asked me to stop, but he didn't have to.

Each time I got high, I found myself wanting to break up with Nick. The drugs I took made sure my inclination toward sabotaging what was good in my life continued. My reasoning, if you could call it that, was that since drugs were considered to be a truth serum, I must really want to break up with Nick if I felt that way each time I was high. It took me a while to realise it was the paranoia the drugs created that made me feel like ending the relationship with Nick.

As much as I tried to push him away, I didn't actually walk away from him. The fact was, I couldn't walk away from him. I was drawn to him as much as he was to me. That's when I started to question the drugs. But ending that long love affair was harder than I imagined. Like many other addicts, I'd discovered, with the drugs inside me, I felt like I had free rein to do as I pleased.

At the club, I threw myself into the music, letting my singing and dancing get lifted to a whole new level. I swayed and danced with abandon. Dancing was my release. It gave me a feeling of emancipation from the past and from everything that had gone wrong in my life. Without drugs though, the throbbing music did nothing for me. Without drugs, I couldn't be transported to that zone of euphoria that seemed to make my troubles melt away. Drugs were the crutch I needed to stay alive and, despite the happiness I felt in other parts of my life, I still wasn't ready to stand on my own two feet.

I managed to persevere with my new, clean outlook on life for a few months, before slipping back to my old ways again. A few months later, the crushing weight of depression convinced me that drugs were stifling me. Squeezing the joy out of my life. I hated what I was doing to myself and resolved to never take drugs again. It was tough, but I succeeded this time. I felt like I was born again.

LOVING AGAIN

2004–2007

One thing that bugged me about Nick was, he wasn't overly demonstrative of his feelings for me, not even once in a while. I often felt like he was simply going through the motions and I wanted to feel more.

Nick told me he loved me and we often discussed marriage and a future together, but he never looked at me with puppy-dog eyes, overflowing with love. At the time, probably because my craving for feeling truly loved had been so desperate for so very long, I wondered why he couldn't do that. Why wouldn't he show his love for me openly and without any self-conscious inhibition?

Looking back now, I can see this criticism of him was another one of my attempts to detect some weakness or failing in him.

One thing he never hesitated to demonstrate was how protective he was of me. Once, he accompanied me while I dropped Adam to Gaz at a mutually agreed location. Gaz and I spoke for a few moments about Adam's needs and where we would meet when he had to return Adam to me. Nick had been hanging back but, suddenly, as our words turned into a heated argument, he appeared by my side, and at my defence.

'Hey, you will not speak to her like that anymore,' Nick said. 'You treat her with respect or you deal with me!'

Gaz backed down and walked away. I couldn't stop smiling at Nick all the way home. It felt good to no longer fear Gaz and it felt even better that Nick was unwavering in his support of me and Adam. After that, I started focusing only on Nick's positives, rather than seeking out his faults. We'd been dating for seven months when I went to Malaysia with Adam to visit my family. Daddy and Nick came to the airport to see us off and we were chatting casually to pass time in the queue as Adam and I waited to board, when Nick asked me the question I'd been thinking about a lot.

'How about us starting a life together?'

It felt like my heart would beat out of my chest.

'Are you proposing? Of course, yes, yes! I want to!'

The flight was a whirlwind of emotions for me but reality set in again when my holiday was over and I returned to Nick and his unhappy mother. She'd brought him up as a single mother after Nick's father walked away during her pregnancy. I was aware she was carrying the trauma of receiving no support and no acknowledgment of their son's existence. My mother-in-law had already lost her partner. She didn't want to lose her son and was trying to protect him in whatever way she could. But banging her hand repeatedly against her head, as a response to the news that Nick and I loved each other and wanted to get married, was not a happy beginning to a positive relationship with my future mother-in-law.

'I wanted to gain a family, not destroy one.' I slipped off my engagement ring, placed it in her hand and walked out of her house.

Nick followed me outside. 'How could you be so rude to my mother?'

Seeing how upset he was, I felt guilty about giving back the ring. But I really wanted to marry him. So, when he asked me to come back in, I went into the house and apologised to his mum.

For a long time, she kept crying and crying and I helplessly kept whispering that I was sorry.

Gaz hurt me every time he hit me. But people can also hurt you without physical blows. Nick's mum might not have punched me or done me any physical harm, but seeing how upset she was about Nick marrying an individual from an Indian background, diverging from the envisioned ideal of a Greek Orthodox Christian she had pictured for him, was equally distressing.

I hadn't set any conditions, religious or otherwise, when I got married to Gaz. I didn't want to make the same mistake again. A relationship like marriage needs to be between two equals. I had to do what I felt was right to ensure my relationship with Nick grew stronger and, more importantly, that I drew individual strength and confidence from it too.

The entire time I'd been floundering in that deep pit of desolation, one of the lifelines I'd clung to was Adam. As his mother, it was more important to live, than die. My other critical lifeline was Islam.

My spiritual beliefs are important to me. I'd turned my back on them when things were at their worst. But now, I was gaining strength from them and they helped me set the boundaries, the conditions, that were vital for me and the success of my relationship with Nick.

Nick's family insisted on a traditional Greek Orthodox wedding, while I felt very strongly that I couldn't continue to be with Nick if we didn't follow certain personal beliefs and traditions important to me. However, both of us knew that, even though our religious backgrounds were different, we both believed in the same kind of love. Love that was pure, non-judgemental and accepting. Nick already had a basic understanding of the principles of Islam. He fully understood my feelings when I explained them to him and didn't hesitate to embrace my traditions and faith to show how much his love and respect for me meant to him.

After reading a book about my spiritual beliefs, Nick asked my father and the Imam to witness his acceptance of my faith. As part of the procedure, he was asked if he understood what he was about to do and if he was being forced into it.

Daddy was so proud that Nick had asked him to witness his acceptance of my spirituality. As expected, Nick's family, being devout Greek Orthodox, wasn't happy about him accepting my faith. Planning a wonderful Greek Orthodox church wedding would take a lot of work, so we agreed to have that in about a year but, five months after Nick proposed, I started planning the Islamic wedding – our Nikah.

We decided to have it on a Saturday and set the date for our Greek Orthodox wedding on the first anniversary of this day.

I knew that even after his conversion, Nick would still follow the Greek Orthodox way of life that he had been raised to be part of and I was fine with that. He was his mother's only son and I could appreciate the power in that relationship and how much it would hurt her if her son totally disregarded the faith in which he'd been raised. In return though, I knew his family didn't give my religious beliefs the same consideration. I pushed through those feelings by reminding myself that I was marrying Nick, not them. His actions were all that mattered.

The pressure he was facing though, started to leave an impact on him and his attitude to our Islamic ceremony. He started teasing me about the formalities of our special day, as if the Nikah was all my responsibility and he was just playing a part. His attitude hurt me.

On the day, I wore a bright pink sari that Mummy had worn for her own wedding ceremony. Gold threads were woven throughout the length of the outfit. A gold scarf covered my hair. My hands and feet were decorated with intricate henna designs and beaded jewellery ran from the scarf to my hairline and across the top of my forehead.

Fifteen Greeks and 100 friends and family from my community attended my parents' house and it was overflowing with people. When Nick and his family arrived, they brought boxes full of gifts. This was the dowry to be presented to the bride's family. Nick's long-time primary school friend, Frank, who was like a brother to him, was very supportive. He took on the responsibility of making sure Nick's family did all they were supposed to do during the course of the ceremony. I hate to imagine how things would've gone if he hadn't been there and I'll always appreciate his help and support at that time. It was especially important to me, because the rest of Nick's family milled around at the back of the room and didn't mingle with my family.

The ceremony started as soon as Nick arrived. My little brother, Dane, took off Nick's shoes, as was the custom and then Nick sat on the floor in front of the Imam. A hush descended on our small congregation and the Nikah got underway. Once we exchanged vows before our witnesses and signed the Nikahnama, the marriage contract, the ceremony concluded and Nick and I were married. I then changed into a pretty blue-and-gold sari with real gold threads woven through it. I kept my head bowed and my eyes focused on the ground as I slowly made my way to Nick. I felt a twinge of nervousness as I sat down next to him on the floor, aware that he would soon have to take my scarf off.

Following the traditional custom, I clasped his hand in mine, brought it lovingly to my forehead and said, 'You are my husband.'

Although all the conventional customs were observed during our ceremony, the warm and happy feeling of two families joining together joyfully, was missing. I was hurt that neither my mother-in-law, nor anyone else from Nick's family, told me I was a beautiful bride. But then I reminded myself that witnessing the Indian Muslim ceremony could have been stressful for Nick's mother and that she wasn't being rude by not saying anything to me. Acceptance in action.

For the reception, Mummy had prepared a lavish spread of tantalising dishes—including ten desserts that were both visual and delectable treats. There was no doubting her past as a famous pastry chef in Malaysia.

A year later, the planning of our Greek Orthodox wedding was much more stressful. I had to undergo four months of catechism classes in the evenings before becoming a Greek Orthodox Christian. Nick was very proud of me for agreeing to do this for him. But for me, it was extremely disturbing. One evening, when I burst out crying, the priest asked me what was wrong and I blurted out, 'Nick converted to Islam when we got married. I can't lie any longer.'

I told him all I'd been through, including the physical abuse, abduction, unhappy marriage and domestic violence and how Nick was such a huge part of my new life and I didn't want to give him up.

'I will never raise my children to be Greek Orthodox,' I told him. 'I'm only doing this for my mother-in-law's sake, because I believe she needs her dreams for her son to be acknowledged and respected.'

He looked at me and said, 'Your kindness toward what is important for your mother-in-law and your honesty in expressing the truth of your marriage, show me that you are an honourable person. I am happy to perform your wedding ceremony in the Greek Orthodox Church.'

Knowing the priest knew the truth, made me feel so relieved and much more comfortable marrying Nick. Nick's family were also more at ease when it was time for our Greek Orthodox wedding. We had five bridesmaids and groomsmen. I was proud to have Jocelyn as one of my bridesmaids. She was the one who wiped my tears and comforted me through the dark days of my marriage to Gaz and our attachment to each other since our school days was genuine and mutually caring. There was no doubting her love for me and I will never forget the many times she stood in steadfast support of me.

My wedding dress, which I'd bought from a second-hand store to save money, was made of ivory silk, with delicate, embroidered lace on the bodice and train. It looked like a dream. I got a tailor to hand-stitch Swarovski crystals all over the dress and also embellish the front of the skirt with more of them. The train of the dress could be hooked up at the back to make dancing much easier.

On our wedding day, we enjoyed a beautiful ceremony in the Greek Orthodox Church. Even Jocelyn seemed to have finally accepted Nick as my husband. This time, there were about eight people from my community and 200 Greeks for the wedding. I couldn't believe it was really happening. Was I really marrying the man of my dreams?

But even the most beautiful dreams have difficult moments. As Nick and I began to settle into our new life together, I discovered a few members of his family were finding it hard to understand the way I did things, mostly when it came to my adherence to some religious and cultural customs.

One day, soon after our Greek wedding, when his cousin

came to visit, I requested she take her shoes off at the door of our apartment and come in. When she asked why, I said, 'Because this is our Asian culture.'

She then turned to Nick and said, 'Oh, aren't you a good Asian boy?'

It could have been a joke on her part, but to me it signified a lack of respect for Nick and me and our home. I don't know if my inference was right or the stress of his family's disapproval of me had made me over-react, but I can now see, to a Greek family, my Asian and spiritual customs must have come across as strange and perplexing. There was another stress, too. I was having trouble conceiving.

Nick and I were so keen to raise a family that we'd started trying to have a baby soon after the first ceremony and I didn't think it would take us long to have one on the way. We'd tried everything and had even enrolled in a course about ovulation and correct consummation timing. Nothing had worked. After nearly a year of trying unsuccessfully, we made an appointment with an IVF clinic. I dreaded being told that drugs and alcohol had caused permanent damage and I'd never be able to have children. Thankfully, nothing like that eventuated but, with our wedding approaching, we chose to put the treatment on hold, temporarily.

Luckily for us, nature had its own plans for us, anyway.

We finally received the good news we'd been eagerly waiting for and it was made even sweeter by finding out when we were on our family honeymoon at Hayman Island with Adam. Admittedly, the timing was a little awkward, considering we'd just had our Greek Orthodox wedding only a few days before, but Nick and I knew the bond we shared was rock solid and were past caring about what others thought about us.

I was over the moon to find out I was pregnant. There was

nothing more I wanted than to have Nick's baby. I knew the new family we were creating was going to be the most supportive and loving environment for a baby to be born into. Finding out its gender and imagining it as a growing mini human, made it even more exciting. I was going to give birth to a little boy – my little King Alexii. He would be a little Eurasian-Greek-Indian-Malaysian bundle of multicultural joy. I knew Adam would be the best brother to his sibling.

Nick looked at me with such adoring eyes, and was so caring towards Adam, that I never doubted we would be the perfect little family. I felt like I was the luckiest woman in the world. Mummy continued to go back and forth between Malaysia and Australia as she planned for a life after retirement back in Malaysia with Daddy. But now, she had her own painful reality to face and when I answered my phone to the sound of her desolate sobs, it was clear her days of living in denial were over.

'I'm leaving your father. He's had that woman living in our house while I was gone. I've just thrown all your father's stuff outside the house. I want a divorce, Liza. I want it now!'

I'd had previous conversations with Mummy about Norida and Daddy but this time it looked like she was determined to divorce him. I only wished she'd had the courage to do this much earlier, when her children were small. Instead, despite knowing he had a mistress, she'd continued to stay with Daddy because of her kids and societal pressures. Or maybe the real reason was because she still loved him.

I promised to take Mummy to a good lawyer, a wonderful Greek gentleman who'd been helping me with Adam's custody arrangements. Then, not long after calming Mummy down, my phone rang again. This time it was Daddy crying to me that Mummy had kicked him out of the house.

'I've nowhere to go. Can I stay with you, Liza?' He sounded agitated.

If only he'd had the guts to divorce Mummy years ago, perhaps all of us would've led happier lives. I felt caught in the middle. Neither of my parents had ever stopped to think about how their muddled decisions impacted their children. Now, they needed my help to sort things out. Daddy was able to stay with one of Mummy's good friends who'd been supporting Daddy's relationship with Norida behind her back. I took Mummy to the lawyer and got the divorce proceedings started. After that, she went back to Malaysia.

Mummy and Daddy would finally get their divorce and get on with their lives away from each other. For me and my life, however, it would be a while before everything was calm and under control. Despite my happy marriage with Nick, it still seemed like a jigsaw puzzle with pieces missing. I bought my first tailoring store on Spencer Street with the intention of expanding and branding Nick's tailoring business. I suggested we change the original name from South Yarra Alterations to Finest Alterations to give the business an image makeover. It worked. The new name brought in more clients and managing my own store gave my confidence a huge boost.

I finally felt in control of some of the most fundamental aspects of my life and it was making a positive difference. We'd even moved into a house not far from the scene of my abduction in Oxford Street as a proactive way for me to tackle my fears head-on and create happy memories that would help me put past pain behind me and reclaim my future.

Unfortunately, not everything in the family was going as smoothly. Nick's mum continued to be indifferent to me, even after I got pregnant. But it was a different story when we welcomed

Alexii, our little bundle of joy, into the world. He looked just like Nick and my mother-in-law took such a liking to him that she and her new grandson became incredibly close. Fitting in with his family though, continued to be hard work.

I tried my best to be a good daughter-in-law. I included my mother-in-law in everything that we did. I never wanted her to be alone and I tried my best to help her get to know me better.

Throughout my life, I'd grown used to believing the bad or undesirable things that happened to me were my fault. Now, I wondered if I was being unreasonable when I felt Nick wasn't demonstrative enough about his love for me, when Mummy didn't spend as much time with me as I wanted her to, or when Nick's mum didn't appreciate my efforts to be kind to her. Was I only imagining that Nick's mother had a problem with me? Was I being ungrateful for the love I got from Nick and my parents? I didn't have the answers, but I often ended up, not just doubting the intentions of others, but doubting myself as well.

Over time, I found a way to stop getting stressed out over what others could be thinking of me. My way to take back greater control of my own thoughts and good fortune, was to start researching the potential power of manifestation and how we can change what we think of ourselves. I realised, what we think of ourselves should matter more than what others think of us.

Imagine a person getting into a boxing ring, with their gloves up and ready to defend themselves from the first punch that might come their way. That was what I was doing in all my relationships with others, trying to protect myself from potential attacks. I could see I needed to let go of my boxing gloves. Life was safe now. I didn't need to feel so threatened. It took a lot of work. When you live under the shadow of PTSD, the fight-or-flight response in your brain is constantly activated. This was why

I nurtured thoughts of others thinking badly of me. The truth was, they really weren't. It was just my perception.

Understanding the fight-or-flight response automatically triggered in our body to help us cope in dangerous situations, is fascinating. Certain changes, like a higher heart rate and blood pressure to ensure more oxygen reaches the larger muscles, or dilated pupils for seeing better, kick in to protect you in times of genuine danger. But if the fight-or-flight response is set off constantly, even in times of normal day-to-day stress, like when your child is just a few minutes late coming home or you notice a stranger staring at you, then the effect on your mental and physical health can be exhausting. Once I realised this, I began to work on controlling my tendency to identify everything as a threat.

Instead of worrying about what could be going through other people's minds, I started to look inward at who I was. If I liked the person I saw inside me, if I saw she was kind and helpful and honest, then I knew I was not the problem. It was as straightforward as that!

That didn't make it easy, though. It took practice. Many years of low self-esteem, zero self-confidence and inflated levels of self-doubt, weren't easy to overcome. I kept questioning if the extent to which I was being kind and helpful was enough to be considered kind and helpful. It took me a while to learn how to arrest this cycle of endless worrying.

I realised my life was genuinely headed in a good direction. My confidence in myself had grown immensely. I was giving my two children the love and care they deserved. I was no longer addicted to drugs and didn't feel the need to go back to substance abuse. I could honestly say I did my best to be a good wife and mother.

Even so, there were still too many days when life felt like a roller-coaster ride. On some days, it felt like everything was going smoothly and I was enjoying the ride. On others, it felt like things were spinning out of control. On the days when I felt charged with energy, I looked toward the future with confidence and felt upbeat about how far I'd come. But there were also days when I somehow strayed back into the dark times of the past and focused on all the mistakes I'd made, the shameful things I'd done and the lack of courage I'd shown.

Nick and I were out for a Sunday drive without the kids. As we drove through the eastern suburbs of Melbourne, our conversation turned to Gaz. It was annoying the way he always managed to worm his way back into my mind. I was free of him, I knew he could no longer hurt me, yet I still struggled to forget that ugly chapter of my life.

Nick said, 'Why don't you press charges?'

I scoffed at the suggestion.

'Even if I do, who's going to listen? It happened more than five years ago.'

Nick was encouraging.

'You won't know until you try,' he said. 'Whatever the outcome is going to be, this is for you. You need to take control; it is the right thing you need to do for yourself. You didn't do it then, but you need to press charges for yourself now. Some people live as if they didn't get a chance to follow through on what justice they need for themselves. You don't want to live with regret.'

CLOSING AN UGLY CHAPTER

2007–2012

Nick obviously thought there was no better time than the present and pulled the car up outside a large suburban police station.

'Why don't you go in and give it a shot? Maybe they'll listen,' he said.

I shrugged. 'And maybe they won't.'

My previous experiences of seeking justice through the court system had not gone well and I wasn't keen to drag myself through the trauma and humiliation of dealing with defence lawyers who questioned my worth.

A part of me prompted me to simply forget about the terrifying reality of my life with Gaz. It was in the past. Why dig it up? It was done, it was buried. I'd moved on, remarried and had two amazing kids.

'You want me to go through the stress of recounting the horrors of the past? Why can't I just enjoy my life the way it is now? My past life is done. It's finished.'

But Nick was insistent.

'Is it done and finished? Look at how we always end up talking about it. You need closure.'

At that moment, I realised Nick needed closure as much as I did. I hadn't fully understood how hard it was for him to live a contented life with me when my abuser, my brutal ex-husband, had been allowed to get away with what he'd done to me. I had no faith in the legal system, but I trusted Nick's judgement.

'I'll wait in the car,' he said.

Nick knew me so well. He'd understood this was something I needed to do on my own.

I was terribly nervous, but once inside the building, I was surprised by how helpful the staff and police were and how they listened to my story with full attention. When I was told it could take a couple of hours or more to get a statement from me, I called Nick to let him know.

When I returned to the car around three hours later, Nick wanted to know what had happened.

'I didn't think they would, but they're taking the whole thing very seriously,' I said.

I told him about the detailed statement they'd taken from me.

It wasn't long before the helpful detective, who'd been assigned to my case, called me. We went through everything: medical records, medical centres I'd visited, doctors who'd examined and treated me, friends that could testify. This was just the beginning of a very long process.

It took nearly two years to get the closure we both needed. The police had to do their part to ensure the case would stand up in court, so they took their time doing a thorough job of collecting all the evidence they needed.

In the meantime, I followed up with all the medical centres I'd ever been to, asking them to verify the times I'd claimed I was in an abusive relationship and had been assaulted by Gaz. At times, I felt overwhelmed by it all and tired, too. The fact that I got pregnant again during the investigation made me feel even more exhausted. There was so much to do in preparation for the court case, I hardly had any time to enjoy the news that Nick and I would soon be welcoming another child into our family.

I asked my friends if they would come in as witnesses. Some, like Jocelyn and Jihan, agreed immediately. Sadly, not everyone was as helpful. My family in Malaysia were critical of me. They thought I was being unkind, dragging Gaz through the mud and I should just let things go and get on with my life. But the negative reactions didn't unnerve me. I wasn't the same old Liza anymore. I let others think what they wanted to think. In my head, I was clear about what I was doing. I was cleansing myself from the ugliness of the past and was determined to achieve that. Closure is one of the most priceless things you can have in your life. No luxurious possessions or wealth can match what closure can give. Today, I feel proud of having stood up firmly for what was important to me and persisting in seeing my decision through till the very end.

I was nearly seven months pregnant when the case finally came up in court. Finding that the judge was a woman made me feel even more confident. I had Nick and my friends with me for support while I faced Gaz, his parents and his wife, who was sitting next to him, weeping continuously. Like me, she was pregnant. But I had no sympathy for her. She wasn't the victim. I was. I was the one who'd been grievously hurt and I was the one now taking charge of my life.

When I went onto the witness stand, a fresh calmness washed over me. I felt glad I had found the strength to stand up to Gaz that day. I didn't care about the outcome because I knew I was speaking the truth and that it was my truthfulness that would finally set me free. I looked Gaz in the eye as I gave my statement about how he'd belted and battered me for years, how Adam was conceived, not by love, but by rape, how he'd heartlessly threatened to kill my unborn baby with a baseball bat and about the metal plate in my reconstructed face. Once I started, I couldn't stop.

I left the stand feeling triumphant, yet exhausted. I'd suffered a few years of trauma at the hands of Gaz and the investigation of this case I'd filed went on for almost two years. Now, at last! I was going to get some sort of justice. I felt lighter. I also felt a sense of empowerment. I'd just dumped years of pain back onto the man who'd dealt it out to me. His family, who'd protected him all along, were now forced to listen to the harsh truth, which was something they never, ever wanted to acknowledge while it was happening. As for his wife, she was being forewarned of what her life could be like with a husband like Gaz.

Gaz, his lawyer and the police had already had lengthy meetings about the charges he was facing, the likelihood of conviction and the severity of the sentence. Finally, we struck a deal. I didn't want Gaz to face jail time for what he did. That wasn't my objective when I filed the case. I just wanted him to own up, admit to what he'd done and apologise. More than that, I wanted the truth to come out. I didn't and still don't believe in an eye for an eye, or revenge. I believe in forgiveness and closure.

I know that victims of similar crimes could question the willingness to forgive on my part. But frankly, for me, taking Gaz to court was about closure for myself, rather than punishment for him. I believed that, by bringing my perpetrator to court and getting him to admit to his guilt, justice would be served and I could then move on with my life.

When Gaz first entered the courtroom, he'd held his head high and looked at me with that cold-hearted arrogance he'd directed my way so often in the past. By the time he took the stand after me, his arrogance had dissipated considerably. He accepted all the allegations made against him and offered a long statement of apology. He said he was sorry for the trauma and injuries he'd inflicted on me, adding if he could take it back, he would and that he actually did care about me and my family. He also made a special apology to my parents. At times, he seemed to be grovelling like a dog. From thinking he was above the law, he'd finally come down to earth.

I didn't believe he was genuinely sorry, though. I knew the statement was a part of what he had to do to escape going to jail. Still, when it was all over, I left the court feeling joyful, triumphant and immensely satisfied. Taking Gaz to court was my way of openly taking a stand, not just against him, but also against my uncle, my cousin and my abductor. It felt like that grimy carpet, a lifetime of inconvenient facts had been swept under, had finally been lifted. I didn't need to hide my truth anymore.

To hear Gaz pronounced guilty of the charges, including rape, was the most triumphant moment of my life. It was bigger than obtaining a PhD and bigger than being on stage speaking to a packed audience. I was being heard.

On the drive home, I sent up a silent prayer. Maybe I was still worthy of protection. Or was it actually my faith in myself, to not give up seeking the justice that needed to be served, that I needed to believe in more deeply all along? After that, Gaz's contact with Adam dwindled to the point where I was the one trying to ensure Adam maintained a relationship with his father and paternal grandparents. Gaz got busy with his career and his own family and often left it to his wife, Chelsea, to handle the organising of Adam's visits.

Each time I asked Adam if he wanted to see Gaz or his grandparents, he would say, 'No. Why do you keep forcing me to go?'

I felt good about Adam's resistance to these visits and Gaz's lack of interest in seeing Adam. Nick and I had started a family and our third child was on the way. It was important that we all felt part of one family. Having Gaz out of Adam's life would make this even easier.

Adam having my maiden name had never bothered Gaz. But when I let him know, we wanted to change his surname to my married name so he could share the same one as his siblings, he finally agreed. He informed me that he and his family wouldn't be seeing Adam anymore. He didn't tell me why and I didn't ask.

When I broke the news to Adam that he wouldn't be able to see Gaz anymore, he reacted just the way he would have had I told him dinner was going to be 10 minutes late. He just said, 'Okay,' and went back to what he was doing.

We were all very excited the day we changed his name to Pavlakos. I asked Adam to choose where he wanted to go to celebrate the occasion. He chose the Greek deli in South Yarra. I smiled at him, thinking about how far we had come and how much we'd been through to get to that day. Adam officially becoming a Pavlakos was like turning the key in the lock of the door that connected me to the past.

After a little bit of snooping on social media, I found out Gaz had relocated to China. The Gaz chapter in my life was finally closed.

Immediately after I'd agreed to pressing charges against Gaz, Nick and I had taken the kids to Malaysia to visit Mummy. We'd been aware it would be quite some time before the actual court trial started and so we'd taken some time out for the trip. We had a nice time with Mummy. But shortly after our return, she called to say she missed us. The house was quiet without her grandkids, she said, and she kept asking herself why she was in Malaysia when her kids and grandkids were in Melbourne.

We agreed she should come back. The hitch was that her house in Melbourne, the one I'd grown up in, had been sold as part of the divorce settlement. Also, despite Daddy being a successful radiographer, Mummy had received very little from the divorce settlement: just a small lump sum with no claims to his superannuation. Naturally, she was worried about how she could survive.

I had a solution and, even though I was due to give birth any day, I put my plan into action and set up a new, fully furnished home: a tiny rented one-bedroom apartment in South Yarra. It was smaller than what she was used to growing up in the affluent suburbs of Malaysia in a large home with servants and it was a far cry from the three-bedroom home we'd had in Australia together. But when we picked her up from the airport and she stepped inside her own flat, she put a hand to her mouth, and the tears spilled down her cheeks.

'I love it,' she said. 'You promised to sort things out, Liza, and you did it!'

Two days after, she moved in. I went into labour and gave birth to my first daughter, my pride and joy, my cute bundle of delight – Alyana. I'd been longing for a daughter for years and now, I had my own little girl whom I could cuddle and dress just the way I wanted.

Around that same time, Nick, our three kids and I, moved into our new house. Life had been getting busier than ever. By now, we had three tailoring boutiques and could afford a better lifestyle. With Adam in grammar school and a flourishing business, I was ready for the next step, moving to a more peaceful location and into a rented home by the beach.

It was a large, comfortable house, offering stunning views of the sunset and the ocean. Each time I gazed out at the water, I felt elated. I felt free. But the vast and empty ocean, sometimes calm, sometimes rough, revealed other truths. Life too, could be unpredictable and was constantly changing. We just had to find a way to sail through both the good and the bad times.

My relationship with Mummy was steadier now and growing stronger by the day. After I'd helped Nick rebrand his alteration business, Mummy helped run our stores too. Although circumstances had brought us together more closely than ever before, I was still surprised when she delivered an emotional and unexpected apology.

'Liza, I'm so sorry for not being there for you in the past,' she said. 'I did believe you but I didn't have the courage to stand by you. And for that, I ask for your forgiveness.'

Hearing the pain in her voice, I became emotional too. Mummy was now my rock, my constant support. She cooked for me, she helped care for the kids, she went to the shops, everything. I was so glad we were a part of each other's lives now.

In 2011, when my second daughter, Azahra, my little angel, was born, it added to my joy. But life for everyone in the world wasn't always so peaceful.

When the news of the body of a young married woman from a Melbourne suburb was found, raped and murdered, about a week after she'd gone missing, it disturbed me so much that I turned off the TV and walked down to the beach. I took a long walk along the shore, letting the cool water splash against my ankles, until the turmoil in my mind subsided.

'Your death will not be in vain,' I promised her.

I wouldn't let the pain and trauma inflicted on victims like us be forgotten. I made up my mind to write a book to inspire others who'd been through trauma or been abused and disempowered like I once was. I told myself, if I could survive experiences as traumatic as the ones I'd been wrung through and make a new, more beautiful life for myself, then, with the right help, anyone else could too.

But each time I started putting my thoughts down on paper and getting it all out of my head, something would happen to make me change what I wanted to say. What I didn't realise at that time was, I was still healing. I didn't have all the answers, yet.

THE POWER OF REFLECTION

2012–2013

Finally, things seemed okay in my life. No, they were much more than merely okay. I had a caring husband and four wonderful children, my relationship with Mummy had been mended and I'd recently opened one more store in the city, a much bigger one than on Spencer Street.

Learning more about running a business: about lease negotiation, consumer price index, staff management and so many vital aspects of generating profit in a way that's sustainable and smart, became my passion. My previous attempts to study had always been interrupted but now I was in the right frame of mind, driven by genuine motivation and a willingness to grow as a business person, as well as grow my business. The decision to study business management with Nick and then obtain my diploma in franchising, was one of the most focused decisions of my life and the future seemed promising.

Throughout that life-changing period, I'd also started doing something that my heart had been set on years earlier, when I was a confused and dejected teenager wandering around Collins Street. I'd begun shopping at Chanel. I routinely shopped at some other high-end fashion boutiques too but when it came to Chanel, I was a regular customer, so much so, the staff in a few different stores all knew me by name.

One day, as I walked into the store, I found myself wondering,

Does being able to walk into a Chanel store, where the staff know me by name, and purchase whatever I fancy, mean that I've arrived? Does living in a big house by the beach mean that I've arrived?

Nick and I were in the midst of planning a four-week holiday in Europe with our children because I'd always wanted to visit Paris with my family. Does that mean I've arrived? Somehow, this question, Have I arrived? began to gnaw at me. I could see I was always striving to move forward. But I was also striving to make others proud of me. Still always looking for approval and some sort of uninhibited declaration of love and devotion from others. Why was I doing this, despite all the counselling and all the soul-searching?

I found the answer less than a fortnight later. Before I left the local Chanel store that day, the manager told me she would arrange an invitation for me to view the apartment of the late Gabrielle 'Coco' Chanel in Paris, the opulent space within which she'd worked, relaxed, and entertained, while I was in Paris during our holiday in Europe.

There was no denying that I loved buying Chanel handbags and earrings, but I'd never really thought about the woman behind the name, let alone where she'd lived and worked. I'd approached the visit with an attitude of nonchalance. Besides, it wouldn't be my first visit to this particular Chanel store in Paris. I'd been here some years earlier too and tried on clothes five months after the birth of Alyana. At the time, I'd believed I had returned to my pre-baby body quite well. But when I tried on a dress and the sales assistant asked how many months pregnant I was, I felt humiliated and thought it was incredibly insensitive of her. So, this time, I'd walked in there with my emotional armour in place.

A tall, strong-looking, blond woman approached me, smiling.

She carried herself with the grace and style that the Chanel brand is famous for. I introduced myself and she said, 'One moment,' and disappeared into a back room.

An older lady returned.

'Mrs Pavlakos, it's so nice to meet you,' she said, in a thick French accent. 'We're honoured to have you as a guest.'

Coco's apartment wasn't open to the public, she explained. Not everybody received an invite, sometimes not even Chanel VIPs. Realising I'd been given an opportunity to experience something truly special, I looked around me. Suddenly, everything seemed surreal. I started to feel ungrateful for taking the invitation lightly. Frankly, I'd looked toward this visit as a trip to a museum and a chance to get some interior decorating ideas for our own house when we eventually decided to buy one.

I followed the lady up the legendary curved staircase leading to the third-floor apartment.

As we continued up the mirror-lined spiral staircase, multitudes of the Liza that everyone else saw, reflected back at me. Each image revealed the same height and build, the same long dark hair, the same face, with one cheekbone slightly higher than the other. It'd been that way since Gaz had broken my face. I pushed aside the thought of that ugly incident and searched for something else in the mirrors to focus on.

When we stopped on a step, my guide explained, 'This is where Coco Chanel sat and secretly watched her collections being revealed below. This spot allowed her to see the reaction on people's faces as they saw her designs for the first time.'

I stared at the step that looked no different from the others and felt a deeper realisation take hold of me. This wasn't just clever architectural design for people to marvel at. What I was looking at were reflections of Coco Chanel's multifaceted personality.

We continued on up the stairs to the unmarked mirrored door that led into Chanel's private apartment. The ornately decorated room we entered seemed to be bursting with beauty, style and symbolism. It was filled with gilded treasures and fascinating gifts from friends of Coco Chanel, each of which, I was told, was linked to a story.

As I moved about the apartment and took a closer look at Chanel's treasures, I grasped the reality of what her apartment was all about.

Chanel had once said, 'An interior is a natural projection of the soul.'

Her apartment was clearly a projection of not just her soul but her complete persona, her captivating creativity, her brilliant business mind, her streak of boldness, her vulnerabilities, her superstitions.

Wheat sheaf motifs, Chanel's lucky charms and symbols of her rise from an impoverished childhood, were all over the place. And so were the lion statues that indicated her zodiac sign, Leo, and her courage, as well as those famous interlocked double Cs for her name and representations of her lucky number five. Glittering crystal chandeliers stood as a testimony to her steadfast belief in the healing powers of crystal.

The oversized beige couch in the room was a distinctive reminder of Chanel's bold sense of style. Instead of velvet or silk, the traditionally preferred materials for furniture in those days, she'd picked an unconventional material like suede.

I'd no doubt Chanel was a strong and independent-minded woman, but still, I sensed loneliness in the midst of all the lavishness on display. I wondered if the beautiful objects Chanel had surrounded herself with were things she treasured or if they just served to distract her from something deeply disturbing in her life, much like I'd tried to divert my attention from my uneven cheekbones and the painful memories they evoked in me.

I wondered what Coco Chanel would have said to me if she were there in the room. And then, it seemed as if from the depths of her treasures, she was whispering, No, you're not insignificant. What you have achieved is worthy of applause and admiration. You are worthy of applause and admiration. And respect.

I'd come a long way from the 15-year-old Liza and those many occasions I'd gazed wistfully into the Melbourne Chanel store window, dreaming of a life filled with love, instead of abuse and mistrust. Yet, despite running successful businesses, I still hadn't thought much of myself or what I'd achieved. I'd never given myself credit for the amount of work that went into raising four children. I'd never for a moment paused to think how amazing this was.

It was time to acknowledge my self-worth. Time for a little self-love. If I'd seemed a little lackadaisical when I entered the Chanel store, I was feeling on top of the world when I left it. I had walked out through the glass doors and onto the pavement outside with just one thought lighting up my mind. I don't need appreciation from others to know my worth. It is enough if I know I am worth it.

TROUBLE IN PARADISE

2013–2015

When Nick planned the holiday in Europe, he hoped it would help me deal with the miscarriage I'd suffered a few weeks earlier. Two months after returning from that holiday, I was elated to find myself pregnant again. But, despite the revitalising burst of joy that the birth of my fifth child, Amira, a real cutie-pie, brought with her, I was beginning to feel a little lost in my marriage. Nick's workload had increased and he seemed to be constantly busy with his determination to grow the alterations business. I was aware we'd taken on a couple of big contracts, but I couldn't help feeling neglected. Thinking about that time, I would also soon have to be back at work, began to stress me out. Part of me wanted to be a permanent stay-at-home mum. But the financial strain of supporting a big family meant I'd have to keep working.

When Amira was three-months-old, Nick and I decided to plan a business trip. Nick was eager to kickstart his own suit tailoring line, so we considered visiting factories in China and Japan. It seemed like a great opportunity to get away – just the three of us.

It was an awesome trip, but just as we were getting ready to leave for Osaka, I began to experience pain in the pelvic region. It was so severe, I could barely walk a few steps. Once back home, we immediately consulted Mummy's oncologist.

After the test results came in, the oncologist told me, in

her opinion, it would be best to get my ovaries removed, as Mum's cancer was hereditary. She advised an oophorectomy and patiently explained what that meant. I was stunned. I already had five beautiful children, so fertility issues were no longer a concern and the relief I felt from knowing the operation would drastically reduce my chances of dying of cancer, was overwhelming. My problem though, was the idea of suddenly losing control of my life again. Would there be more operations? What else would happen to me? In the days before the surgery, I was jittery and in need of constant reassurance. Nick, however, hardly seemed to notice that. Seeing him going about his work as usual made me feel even more tense. Didn't he care about what was happening to me?

As I reflect on those feelings today, I realise it wasn't that Nick did not care, it was simply how he was dealing with his own fears. He was worried about me yet didn't know how to articulate his concern. But because I was feeling such tension about my own future, my brain had shifted into survival mode. I was not thinking clearly.

The cracks in our relationship really started showing when I got admitted into the hospital for my oophorectomy. As I prepared for the operation, on the outside I appeared calm, strong and in control. On the inside, however, I was barely holding it together. I stripped down to my undies and put on the hospital gown. A panicky feeling took hold of me. Was this operation really necessary? What's really going on? Is this really happening to me?

Nick did up the back of my gown and then wrapped his arms around me, to hug me tightly. My reaction surprised him.

'Don't touch me! I'm about to go into surgery! Leave me alone.'

I was afraid and tense and felt like I was going out of my mind. I didn't want the operation. It was pure fear and because I was so worried about the potential outcome, the anxiety I felt, killed any need or desire for affection. But my outburst at poor Nick made me miserable.

At the time, I didn't realise I was letting out my frustration on Nick. His main flaw was that he didn't know how to be present in the marriage. But how could he know any better, when his own father wasn't present in his own life? He never grew up seeing his father shower gifts on his mother, or even simply standing by her side when she was sick and needed care. At least Nick did that for me although, because I was blinded by anger, I didn't focus on those positives.

After the oophorectomy, I shut myself off emotionally from Nick and started sleeping in another room. I went about my work, cooking dinner and mothering our children, but emotionally, I was disconnected from him and our marriage. I was disconnected from myself, my work and my life, too. I didn't enjoy my tailoring business anymore; I felt like I was not in control and, not knowing how to sew, felt like I was at the mercy of my staff. I was severely depressed.

When I started bleeding heavily a couple of weeks later, I was told I'd have to be admitted for a radical hysterectomy, I suddenly felt a shiver of fear run down my spine. What if I am dying? What if, despite the surgeries, the rare cancer gene I've inherited will somehow lead to some other kind of cancer?

I felt time was running out for me. When would I write my book? All the trauma I'd gone through, I didn't want it to be fruitless…worthless. I was desperate for something good to come out of it. I wanted my story to inspire others to success. I didn't want it to be buried or hidden away as if it never happened.

Through my book, to the people who feel intimidated by adversities, I wanted to say, If I could do it, so can you. Life is not an easy journey, but, with conviction, we can overcome anything that stands in our way. You don't need to be voiceless anymore. You should not be silenced any longer. Your history matters and so does your story.

As for my perpetrators, I wanted to tell them, you can't silence me by what you did to me. I'm going to help others because the hate and horror you dished out, inspired me to share love and empathy.

And it wasn't just those in need of motivation that I wanted to help. I wanted my book to be a legacy I'd leave behind for my children and their children. I went in to have the hysterectomy feeling angry as hell. When I was wheeled to my room after coming out of the anaesthetic, Nick was waiting for me. I still had the oxygen mask on and was doped up on morphine. As soon as we were alone, I looked at him and said, 'I want a divorce.'

'Why? I'm here for you, Liza. I love you,' he said, trying to hold my hand.

'No! I don't like the way you treat me. It's because of you that I'm depressed. You're so immersed in your work, you're hardly at home. I don't even know why you married me. Leave me alone. I want to be alone.'

Nick seemed to be on the verge of tears as he looked at me.

'Don't you understand? I love you so much.'

But I was adamant.

'No, I don't. I'm sick of you. If you love me, then just leave me alone. Go away!'

Angry tears streamed down my face. From my perspective, our relationship wasn't just showing cracks, it was being ripped apart.

Nick left and for the next few minutes, I felt lost. Deep in my heart, I didn't want a divorce, but I was severely depressed and didn't want Nick to live with me anymore. I wanted him to get remarried to a Greek Orthodox girl, someone with an uncomplicated life, not someone like me. It would be better if Nick moved on, I told myself. Now, strangely, I felt proud of myself. Proud that I'd been strong enough to ask for a divorce.

I was so upset, it was hard to think rationally. Nick was never going to stand up for me, I convinced myself. It was best to just end the marriage. I realise now how irrational my behaviour was. But I was not just angry with Nick, I was also frustrated by my parents' inability to understand my pain and the traumas I'd suffered. It made me feel like I was unloved and undeserving of love, not even Nick's.

In times of extreme anguish, I tended to cope by escaping from the situation and wanting to be alone. As a teenager, I'd run away from home. Now I wanted to run away from my marriage, as if my brain was constantly in-flight mode.

I began venting my frustration on Nick. But despite my fuming outbursts, he never reacted with anger toward me. Instead, he looked for solutions. When I came home from the hospital, we hired Rosie, a helper and nanny, to look after me during my recovery. She helped with the housework, cared for the kids, cared for me. Rosie was an absolute godsend, doing everything she could to make life easier for me. She brought the joy I needed into my life.

As time went by and I got healthier, Rosie and I would often go to the beach. We would jump off the pier and have loads of fun together. Rosie was somewhat of a hippie. She never cared about how she looked; she cared for nature and the simple things in life. Gradually, being with her began to change me as a person and made me realise there was more to life and that the life I was living was a superficial one. But I still wanted out of my marriage. Every little thing Nick did, irritated me.

Once I recovered from my surgeries, I immediately turned my attention to my book. I knew I would need guts to bare my soul and thinking back to the past would take me to some dark, ugly spaces in my memory. I didn't let that deter me. I was ready to put everything down on paper. I spent some time drawing up a rough outline and then, my mind buzzing with all the things I wanted to say, I launched into the process of transforming my thoughts into words.

In those early stages, members of my family seemed to encourage me. I think that was because they thought it would never get published. Maybe they thought writing everything down would help get all the painful memories out of my system, and then I would forget all about the book and get on with my life. As I continued with the writing, I got the feeling they weren't taking what I was doing as seriously as they should.

Nick seemed to be supportive and that was amazing on his part. But he was reluctant to read anything that I'd written. I soon realised he was afraid of finding my book too uncomfortable to read.

By now, I'd also decided to open our fifth store in the heart of Melbourne CBD and Nick and I would take time to go out for dinners more often. But I'd often find myself spoiling the mood by saying, 'Why are you still married to me? Don't you think your life would've been better with someone else, someone whose life was less complicated?'

I soon realised these things were coming out of me because I'd totally shut down from Nick. I couldn't see myself ever finding my way back to him. I was in a marriage where I wasn't happy anymore. Even at our stores, despite being in the business for almost a decade, every time I served a customer, I felt like I didn't believe in what I was selling. At home too, even with five beautiful kids, my life felt empty. Every time I turned on the TV and heard about another woman being killed or another child being abducted, I could feel the pain of the victim. It felt like every moment was triggering uncomfortable thoughts in my mind and my life was caving in on me. Nick, however, persisted and hung in there.

To help us get back on track as a family unit, we decided it was time we lived in a house we owned, so I sold off two of my alteration stores and used the money to put down a deposit on a spacious house just a kilometre from the beach in Beaumaris. The house sat on a large block of land and had ample space in front and all around it. The children's school was just a short stroll away. Nick was okay with the move. But although he and I were still together, I'd only put my name on the house title. I wanted to protect myself and protect my financial independence.

Then one day, Mummy dropped a bombshell on me. Until then, she'd been travelling back and forth between Malaysia and Australia quite a bit. I'd thought she was happy in Australia, so was shocked by her decision to relocate permanently back to Malaysia.

To add to the shock announcement, there was the complication of Mummy's home. Only a few months earlier, even before I'd bought my own house in Beaumaris, my godmother in Malaysia and I had pooled together our money to buy a house for Mummy in Melbourne, a short distance from where I now lived. The house was in my name and the purchase was a good investment. Now, though, it would have to be sold but selling it within a year at a loss meant we couldn't give my mum any proceeds. This strained our relationship.

I started to hear that my mother was spreading a lot of stories about me and I couldn't believe it. One story said she was working as a maid in my stores while taking care of my kids. That couldn't be further from the truth. She had everything she needed and she loved spending time with her grandchildren.

I talked to my mother about what I'd heard and she said it was all lies. It wasn't just one person warning me about her and what she was saying, it was five of her friends, all telling me the same things and it hurt so much. But I wanted to believe my mother more than anyone else. After all, we had a strong bond and I was her devoted daughter who did everything to support her.

Soon, we were hardly communicating. Now, I was really going to be alone, I thought. Estranged from Nick and from Mummy as well.

Two days before she was due to leave, I called her to ask about her flight. I didn't want her to leave without even saying goodbye.

'My flight is at night,' she said, 'but don't worry about it, Aunty Sandy is going to take me to the airport.'

I was mortified. And angry. I talked to Daddy.

'Can you believe that Mummy's leaving?' I said. 'And she's not even communicating with me like before. I don't understand it.'

'Let her be,' Daddy said. 'Let her live her life.'

A little later, Mummy called and asked me to pick the children up from school the next day in the afternoon and bring them to her house. That way she would get to say goodbye to them and me before she left, she said. I did what she asked. Everything in the house was pretty much gone. It was exactly how I felt inside. Empty. My chest hurt. I suggested Mummy sleep at my house the night before she left. But she had too much pride. She still felt I'd cheated her by not giving her anything from the sale of the house. She also felt she needed to live her own life in Malaysia.

She migrated here to start a life with my father and he consistently distorted her reality by cheating on her when he was supposedly faithfully married. While he was married, he had another child with Norida. Mummy felt used and isolated – to her core! And, no matter how much I craved and loved her, she wanted to finally live her life her way, to make up for feeling that her life had been forever sacrificed for others. When it came to the finances connected to the sale of that property, though, what she didn't understand was there was nothing to give back to her. All the money had to be used to settle the debts: stamp duty, lenders' mortgage insurance and taxes incurred in buying the house. My mother had hoped to use the sales proceeds to repay my godmother, who had put a deposit towards the house. The truth was, there was nothing to give back; everyone—my godmother and me—lost financially.

The children hugged her, one by one. Then it was my turn.

'Bye, Mummy. Take care. I'll come and see you soon.'

'Thank you, Liza, for letting me go, letting me do what I have to do,' she said after a long pause.

Our conversation was stilted, like we both had so much to say but were holding back.

'That's okay, Mummy,' I said, immediately reacting like the old Liza again. 'I want you to be happy. That's all I want for you.'

I was still upset with her. I didn't want her to die somewhere miles away. I wouldn't be able to bear it if she suddenly got sick again and I wasn't able to rush to her, to be by her side and take care of her.

HANOVER HOUSE

2015

By now, I was over feeling depressed about my unexpected surgeries and being disappointed in Nick for not measuring up to my expectations. But a strange feeling of discontent still lingered within me. Nick and I spent time with our children together whenever we could, had fun together as a family and still dined out occasionally, but somehow, I felt as though something was missing. I'd been excited about finally moving into a house I owned. So now, why was I feeling low? Why couldn't I dispel the restlessness? Was I expecting too much from my marriage? From Nick? I could see he kept trying to put me at ease and I appreciated the efforts he made to keep our marriage stable.

The problem was with me, I decided. My life was good. Yet it was as if I couldn't stand any more of it. I had so many things to be proud of and grateful for. A lovely family, an upscale home in Melbourne by the sea, wealth, a good life. I had it all. I was a successful businesswoman with a loving, supportive husband and five beautiful children. Could anyone in their right senses want anything more?

I have to admit, though, that I seemed to be constantly worrying about money, about earning more to keep our business going and my family comfortable. I also tended to focus on distressing, negative things. The size of our mortgage, the mounting bills, the hassles of dealing with disgruntled customers, escalating business costs, a client base that wasn't expanding fast enough. Sometimes it felt as if I had no choice but to be a part of the never-ending, nerve-wracking rat race.

I felt frustrated. I felt stuck. I wondered what I could do to change or at least improve my situation. I decided I needed a sort of in-my-face reminder of how good my life was now. That was when I remembered Hanover House, a shelter for homeless women in East St. Kilda. It was run by an independent organisation offering housing and support to the homeless.

Nick had introduced me to Hanover years ago, even before we got married. He was a volunteer at their site in South Melbourne that provided crisis accommodation to families. Every Sunday he would assist in cooking the barbecue for the residents. When we started dating, I joined him in his volunteer work. And when Adam was old enough, he began to help out too. I'd make salads and Adam would help set out the drinks. I remembered what a wonderful experience that was.

I considered volunteering with Hanover again but at their shelter for women. Perhaps working with people whose lives were not as good as mine and helping them feel happy and secure again, would make me look at my own life differently, I thought. Besides, I knew what it was like to be homeless, to be abused and to feel powerless. That would certainly make it easier for me to empathise with these women, serve them better.

One night, I discussed this with Nick.

'That would be good,' he said, 'if you can spare the time. You've already contacted them?'

I said, 'No. I'm going to call them tomorrow.'

Luckily for me, they were taking on volunteers. But I was told things were different now. I couldn't just turn up and start assisting them like before. The recruitment process was now more in-depth. Interviewee reference checks, police checks and a "Working with Children" check would need to be done. All in strict confidence, of course. I arranged for these to be taken care of and filled out the required paperwork using my letterhead, clearly indicating my professional designation as director of our chain of clothes alteration stores. Soon, a lady named Chloe phoned me, asking me to come in for an interview.

I had no babysitter for the day of the interview. So, I took all five children with me: Adam (16), Alexii (8), Alyana (6), Azahra (4), and Amira (1). I knew it wasn't normal for an interviewee to turn up with all their children in tow, at Hanover or any other organisation, but that didn't stop me. This is me, I thought. This is a big part of who I am. I'm doing what I have to do so I can make it for the interview.

The surprised look on Chloe's face, when she glanced at our little group standing at her office door, said it all. Even so, we proceeded with the interview.

I requested the children to be quiet as we entered Chloe's office. The boys and Alyana played unobtrusively in one corner and my youngest two kids sat on my lap.

When Chloe asked me what I did, I explained about the alteration stores Nick and I owned and managed, also adding, 'I'm in the process of writing my first book.'

That interested her a lot. 'What is it about?'

'It's about adversity, life after trauma and finding a way to move forward, all based on my own experiences,' I said.

Chloe asked what those experiences were. After I opened up about the abuse and traumatic events in my life, she said, 'It's amazing you can talk so easily about all of this. How about running a writing workshop? For traumatised women struggling to overcome personal problems.'

And so, three weeks later, on a cold, rain-soaked night, I set off for the Hanover shelter in East St. Kilda

'Hi, I'm Liza. I'm here for the writing workshop,' I told the lady who answered the door. I signed in and followed her into the lounge.

I was a little nervous about not having brought along anything with me by way of stationery or props. I hadn't even planned the lesson. She handed me some pens and paper for the students.

'We have six women attending your class tonight,' she said and left.

Six women! How will I handle six women? Before I could give this another thought, a young woman walked in and sat at the table. She wore jeans with an unbuttoned red plaid shirt over a t-shirt. She had short hair and beautiful eyes and seemed like a pretty girl trying to hide behind a tough-boy look.

'Hi,' I said. 'You're here for the writing workshop?'

She nodded. Her name was Chelsea and she was there because she loved to write. Her answer helped calm my nerves. However, despite her obvious enthusiasm for the class, she seemed lost, as if unsure about truly fitting into any group, not even the writing group she'd chosen to join.

I tried to get her to talk to me. But when she did, she startled me by saying she believed the earth would explode in 100 years and she was going to live for another 80 years. She said this with a calm confidence. It was obvious to me the peculiar way her mind was working was a consequence of the ordeals she'd been through. Trauma affects people differently and this was how it had affected her.

Soon afterward, the other five students arrived and joined us. I smiled, introduced myself and said, 'I'm here to help you write. Do you know what you would like to write about?'

The women shook their heads. By now, the room was insufferably hot to me. My hormones had kick-started a hot flush. I routinely had to contend with this after the oophorectomy and the radical hysterectomy. I was tempted to ask for the heating to be turned down, but the girls didn't seem to be bothered about the heat, so I left it. I was more concerned about them being as comfortable as possible.

'I haven't planned a lesson,' I said. 'Thought it would be better if we figured it out after we met. But how about me first telling you a little about myself?'

The expressions on the girls' faces told me they were keen to hear my story. I told them about myself, beginning with my early childhood and the first traumatic experience of my life – being sexually abused by my own uncle. I stopped after relating this and asked if they wanted me to go on. I was afraid what I'd just narrated could've upset them. The last thing I wanted to do was reopen old wounds of their own painful pasts.

On the contrary, the women were unanimous in their request to hear more of my experiences. So, I continued sharing more and more of my story, stopping now and then to check they still wanted to hear more until I got to one of the most painful incidents in my life.

'And then, when I least expected it, I was abducted. I'm not sure if I should—'

'Abducted? This is crazy!' Chelsea said. 'It's like a scene from CSI Miami!'

The women seemed moved that I was anxious about my experiences not stressing them out in any way but requested me to continue. I went on to tell them how this and other adversities had come my way, but emphasised that, rather than being intimidated by the things holding me back, I'd finally found the inner strength to overcome them. I chose to overcome them. Not just that, I'd successfully started several of my own businesses and now had a loving, supportive husband and five lovely children. I finished off with a positive message for them.

'Remember, it's not the adversities in our life that define us; it's how we choose to handle those challenges that defines us. My own life is proof of this.'

I gave them a few moments to mull over all that I'd shared with them and launched into the writing lesson.

'Writing is a great way to express our feelings. Any feelings. So, let's start by writing about feelings. It could be about anything you've been through.'

Colleen wrote a poignant love song, beautifully expressing what she felt in her heart. Lisa said she wanted to attempt writing a novel. Another pleasant surprise was Chelsea setting out to write a science-fiction type of story. The class was supposed to go on for only one hour. But by the time I left the shelter that night, three hours had passed. When I reached home, despite the exhaustion, I felt exhilarated.

My first day at the homeless shelter had revealed a basic but crucial truth to me. Something so wonderfully captured in that line from the famed prayer of St. Francis of Assisi:

For it is in giving that we receive.

It didn't matter how much money I made or how wonderful a lifestyle I lived. None of it would make me feel as happy as reaching out and making someone else happy by making a difference in their life. I knew many of the women in my writing class would be with me for just a few days before the organisation moved them to more permanent accommodation. So, I focused on making a change in their lives from their first day, no matter how small.

Even after Chelsea left my class, I often thought about her and how lost she'd seemed when I first met her. After her first lesson, she'd slowly opened up to me, disclosing how she'd been in foster care ever since she was a baby and been moved from house to house, sometimes neglected, sometimes abused. Although we came from two very different worlds, I could relate to the loneliness of her childhood. During the time she attended my class, she seemed more relaxed and ended up writing four pages of her science-fiction story.

Meeting her served as a stark reminder of how far I'd come from the disempowered, terrified person I once was. The women in my class had seemed stunned by the immensity of the trauma I'd suffered and survived. But that was not my goal. I wasn't seeking their admiration. What I wanted was to inspire them to surmount the obstacles that were holding them back.

At first, baring my soul and telling my story to strangers wasn't easy. But I knew I had to do this to make those women see that I was once a victim like them. In many ways, I understood their pain. I knew the narrative of my life must come across as a horror story, one ghastly incident following the other. And when it came to my abduction, even to my own ears my story sounded far-fetched. However, it made me happy to reveal there was a bright side to my story as well. It was immensely satisfying to know that by showing the women in the homeless shelter how the worst adversities could be overcome, I was, in a way, empowering them to take control of their lives as well.

REDISCOVERING LOVE AND RECOGNISING SIGNS

2015

When Nick encouraged me to attend an event run by the amazing motivational speaker, Dr Wayne Dyer, I was happy I took his advice. Today, I look back on that decision as my own light-bulb moment – a genuine sign.

When I decided to attend that two-day seminar, in August 2015, I'd just wound up my volunteer work at Hanover House. On the one hand, I was upbeat about the way relating my story had motivated the traumatised young women at the homeless shelter, but on the other, I felt like I was at a dead-end. I didn't know what to do with the knowledge I'd gained about my ability to inspire others. I hadn't yet recognised my purpose was to become an impactful motivational speaker. Yet, I felt drawn to Dr Dyer's presence in my own city and I am grateful that Nick encouraged and motivated me to actually attend.

It was a decision I have never regretted. Dr Dyer was as engaging and charismatic as I expected and the whole audience, including me, was spellbound. For me, the experience was sublime. On the first day, as I listened to his daughter, Skye Dyer, singing the India Arie number, I am Light, I felt as if she was singing the song especially for me. The powerful lyrics held so much meaning for me and made me realise, no matter how broken I might feel, I have light within me. And that light can shine so radiantly.

I realised I might not be able to speak to him personally, but Dr Dyer's words left such an impact on me that I sent an email to his daughter that night, mentioning how much I enjoyed listening to her sing. I introduced myself, explained a little of my own experiences and why it was so important to me to inspire and help others and told her how keen I was to meet her father. I kept my fingers crossed, hoping she would pass on my message. I knew I was not the only one with such a wish. Still, it was worth a try.

At the end of the seminar, the queue of people lining up to have a personal interaction with Dr Dyer was so long that I wondered if the organisers would allow all the fans to even shake his hand, let alone have any meaningful conversation.

One of the women I'd become friendly with at the seminar, Louisa, seemed even more disappointed than I was. We exchanged numbers, told each other how wonderful it would be to meet again, then said goodbye. I loitered around for a while, watching the people jostling to meet him, but then left the venue. The Hilton Hotel was a 15-minute walk away and I was looking for a spacious bathroom, where I could take the time to do my hair and makeup without being rushed, before I headed home. As a busy mother of five, I rarely got enough time for such self-indulgence and taking my time, while I thought over everything I'd seen and heard at the seminar, was a treat.

When I stepped out, I was stunned to see Dr Dyer, waiting patiently for his own turn to use the bathroom. For a few awkward seconds, I was too stunned to say anything. The situation was so surreal. Only the previous night I'd written a letter to his daughter requesting her to tell her father I badly wanted to meet him and now here I was face-to-face with the man himself. Here was my opportunity to tell him about myself, my life, my need for guidance and my desire to motivate others just like he did. But, standing outside the bathroom I felt the time to tell him that was not appropriate, so I didn't.

Instead, I told him I'd attended his seminar and a woman I'd befriended had been desperate to talk to him and have her photo taken with him. I asked if he could speak a few words to her and he very graciously agreed! So, I dialled Louisa's number and handed my phone to him. After he talked to her, I thanked him and was about to leave when he stopped me. He wanted to know my name and asked if I didn't want to have my photo taken with him. I couldn't believe my ears.

I left the Hilton feeling on top of the world. I saw the totally unexpected meeting with such a successful international speaker as a powerful sign that I was meant to forge my own path in the same field. I felt as if a higher power was at work, pointing me toward the career journey I was born to explore.

Just six days later, Dr Dyer passed away at his home in Hawaii. I was deeply saddened by the news but so glad I'd made the decision to attend his last seminar and even meet him in person. I sent Skye Dyer a condolence letter, along with a copy of my photo with her father. I was so thankful for having met her dad, I told her. Attending his seminar and meeting him had let me discover my calling. Pursuing that calling has changed my life.

I am Light was an incredible two-day workshop that helped me understand how freeing myself from negative thoughts would change the way I looked at a situation and change the way I interacted with loved ones and others. Dr Dyer's words truly lifted me up, revealing how I could live a purposeful life. I came away from the event fired up by the determination to stay positive, no matter what and to touch the lives of others positively, just like he did. To shine a light for others, just like he did. My purpose was to become a motivational speaker to help others.

At the same time, this goal was underpinned by the knowledge of what being a motivational speaker could do for me. All those times when I'd been abused as a voiceless, powerless victim, it was like I was passively having my backside kicked, without making even the feeblest attempt to protect myself, let alone hit back at the abusers. By telling my story as a motivational speaker, I would be doing more than just helping others triumph over their own unique trauma and adversities. I would be getting even with my past tormentors, but in a positive way.

The first thing I did toward achieving my new goal, was engage a husband-wife team to create a road map for me to become a professional motivational speaker. I told them everything about my life, the trauma I'd endured and how I'd motivated myself to overcome the challenges I was faced with.

The business plan they designed for me kicked off with meeting a professor at the University of Melbourne, Dr Berhan Ahmed, who was also the chairperson of the Family Violence Conference organising committee at that time. When I talked to him about my own experiences, he invited me to speak at the Family Violence Conference to be held at their Parkville campus the following month. I was overjoyed. I hadn't expected to be booked for my first speaking engagement so soon. I had a month to prepare for it and got busy making the initial notes. The very next morning, though, Nick and I were leaving for a week-long holiday in the Maldives.

We'd been planning the trip before my health scare and the subsequent surgeries, and with everything that had happened since, Nick felt we should still go. With Mummy back in Australia to enjoy some special time with her grandchildren, Nick and I touched down at our getaway destination.

When I awoke in our hotel room in the morning, I decided to let Nick sleep, while I slipped downstairs to get some breakfast. But by the time I got to the kitchen, I'd decided to make a special breakfast for Nick, myself. He'd brought me all the way to the Maldives to work on our relationship and the least I could do was surprise him with some breakfast.

I peeked into the kitchen through the serving window that separated it from the dining area and was taken aback to see it was a mess. I asked the young guy inside busy cooking breakfast for the guests if I could come inside and help clean the place. He seemed horrified.

'But you're a guest.'

I had a hunch the cabinets were as untidy as the kitchen counters were.

'Yes,' I said, 'but I want to help you. Come on, let's get this party started.'

Minutes later, the rest of the staff trooped in.

By the time I finished with assisting and guiding Mohammed, whose name I'd learned during the clean-up operation, and the other hotel staff, I'd given them lessons in economy, cleanliness and professionalism as well. Nick came downstairs when I was at my busiest in that kitchen and laughed as he tapped me on the shoulder and said, 'I see Liza is busy doing her thing again!'

He'd seen how I had once run the Piccolo Café and knew how well I could take control of a messy situation.

After we had our breakfast, I smiled and said to Mohammed, 'Always remember to take pride in your work, okay? Love your work. If you don't love what you're doing, try and find something else to do that you're passionate about.'

He nodded. 'Thank you, ma'am, for everything. But may I give you a present?'

'A present? Sure.'

Mohammed hurried away and returned with a book that contained the text of the Holy Quran, the New Testament, and the Torah. I stared at the book he held out to me. Was this a sign to me from the divine? It was a heart-warming gift and I thanked him for it. Soon, it was time for us to check out and leave for the Four Seasons.

Mohammed asked if we would like a brief tour of Malé, the capital island of the Maldives, and we agreed. He first took us to the nearby mosque. I went up to the women's section to pray in my hijab. No one else was there, just me. I finished praying and went back downstairs, feeling at peace with myself and the world.

Nick asked if we could get a photograph of us taken outside the mosque. He stood proudly and happily next to me, his Indian Malaysian wife, while we had it taken. I was still in my hijab. I wished he'd been like this back in Australia when that relative of his had visited our house soon after we were married.

We took in some sightseeing and, an hour later, were on a speedboat heading to the Four Seasons Resort. It felt like a scene from a James Bond movie. I glanced at Nick and noticed the expression on his face. I realised that neither of us were admiring the view as much as we were seeing each other differently. After a long time, I was rediscovering what a good companion Nick could be. I also thought about my experience at the three-star hotel. Though I knew I could touch people and help them transform their lives into something better, I'd actually seen the results of such a change in Mohammed. From an uninspired, bored and untrained hotel worker, he was now working with a new energy, a new confidence.

When we arrived at the Four Seasons, I finally started looking outward instead of inward. The view literally took my breath away. I'd heard people describe the beauty of the islands, but no description or image could do them justice. If there really was such a thing as heaven on earth, the Maldives was it.

Not only did it look amazing; the experiences were exceptional. The water temperature was like a warm bath. Soothing and refreshing at the same time. We could even swim with sharks that didn't bite and what's more, they didn't trouble us at all.

The next morning, on our third day in the Maldives, Mummy messaged me saying she was getting Rosie, the nanny, to care for the kids during the day because she would be teaching pastry-making at a location around three hours away from Melbourne. The next day she called and said, 'I'm not going to be around. I think it would be best if Rosie just stays and cares for the kids.'

Mummy had let me down badly but when I called Daddy and asked if he could take care of the kids, he assured me he'd love to. I felt so relieved. The circumstance had made me lose all trust in Mummy but brought me closer to Daddy. Nick and I were revelling in a new closeness too.

After arranging separate massages, Nick had told me to meet him for dinner. I thought it was a bit strange, but we'd spent years doing so many things separately that I didn't think too much about it. When I beat him there, I ordered a lychee martini and waited. I'd barely started chatting to one of my girlfriends on Facetime when I received a phone call on the bar phone.

'Mrs Pavlakos, your husband is waiting to have dinner with you.'

I was surprised Nick had gone directly to the restaurant. Was he annoyed because I was late? I quickly asked a buggy to take me there. As I walked toward the restaurant entrance, I noticed the staff and some other guests staring at me. I wondered if something that shouldn't be showing was on public view. A trail of candles had been set out along the path leading to the gazebo at the edge of the restaurant. Nick was inside, sitting at a table overlooking the ocean. The gazebo was lined with candles and soft music was playing in the background. Why was the place all lit up like that?

When I reached Nick, he got to his feet slowly, a shy smile playing on his lips.

'Liza, I never proposed to you properly. Now I want to do it the right way.'

'Okay, what way?'

'You always take control by planning everything. Now, I want to do things my way, the way it should've been done the first time.' Nick got down on one knee and opened the elegant ring box clutched in his hand. He took out a diamond-studded ring from inside and looked up into my face. 'I love you, Liza. You mean everything to me.' Putting the box into his pocket, he slid the ring on my finger. 'Will you marry me? Again?'

I couldn't deny the warm feeling in my heart.

'Nick, we're already married. But yes, I'd love to marry you again.'

We had a beautiful candlelit dinner and celebrated our third wedding (a heartfelt vow renewal that we decided to repeat and formalise, with both my sons walking me down the aisle and both my daughters as flower girls at another celebration, back in Melbourne) in style. Our conversation that night covered many aspects of our future together, but mostly about my wish to become a motivational speaker and my nerves about my upcoming first speaking engagement.

Suddenly, Nick said, 'Why don't you practise your talk?'

I was in holiday relaxation mode and didn't need much coaxing to launch into my act.

'Sure. I'll practise right here.' I stood up and waved a hand in the direction of the three or four staff members hovering around us. 'I'll address the staff of this hotel.'

Nick's encouraging smile fired up my mood even further.

'Hi everyone, my name is Liza and I'm here to tell you that against all odds, you can overcome anything. I stopped and looked at Nick. 'Oh shit, Nick, I've got to do better than that.'

Nick shook his head and smiled. 'No, sweetness. You're doing just fine. Go on. Just do it.'

I noticed the staff had stopped what they were doing and were listening to me. I started again.

'In this world where we live, many things will happen to us that we will not be able to control. My name is Liza and today I'm going to share my story with you. If there is one thing I know, it is that we all have a story to share and that resilience is in all of us. But first, you must ask yourself, are you the victim or the victor of your story? We all have the power to change our lives for the better. To make that happen, you need to tap into your inner strength, focus on staying positive and get ready to work hard. Really hard. And soon, your goals will be within reach.'

The staff started to clap. I thanked them for their appreciation, feeling pleased with myself. I'd never imagined it, but the thought of inspiring people now made me feel as if I was finally fulfilling my purpose in life.

Despite the wonderful time Nick and I had together, I still didn't know what to do with his love when we returned to everyday life back in Melbourne. It felt foreign to me, no matter how much I appreciated his care. The problem was, I wasn't used to receiving so much love and so openly. Especially from Nick. It made me wonder if I really did know what true love felt like and if I knew how to reciprocate such love. I'd spent my entire life craving love, but more than anything, I'd wanted my parents to stand up for me. I wanted to be loved by someone who would put me first, unlike my parents, who'd doubted me and didn't seem to truly understand me.

Why was this happening? I knew I loved him deeply. Then why this sense of being so disconnected from my feelings? It was during a session with my therapist, whom I'd been seeing for some time in a bid to better my state of mind, that I realised I suffered from post-traumatic stress disorder (PTSD) as a side-effect of my past traumas. She told me PTSD could numb a person's feelings and also cause memory loss. For most people, this is a temporary feeling causing a disconnection from their own body and the world around. I wondered if that was why I'd forgotten about the love Nick and I had once shared. Thankfully, my therapist reassured me these feelings and memories can be regained through therapy and time.

One day, she asked me, 'How would you feel if Nick left you and married someone else?'

'That wouldn't bother me,' I said glibly. 'I'd be more than fine with that.'

'How so?'

'Well, we could always co-parent. No matter what, Nick and I would make it work. I'm sure of that. We will always have a good relationship with one another.'

'Okay. But... er... what if Nick passed away? Would you be able to cope with that too?'

The thought of Nick not being in this world shook me. Just the mere thought of being unable to talk to him, see him or touch him ever again, sent an overwhelming sense of loss, loneliness and sadness through me. That's when it hit me. I really, really loved Nick. Maybe we weren't a married couple who did everything together. We weren't joined at the hip, as they say. But we valued what we had. We would fight to preserve what we had.

I realised what I felt for Nick was the true essence of love. I now believe real love is when you love someone so unconditionally you don't mind what path the other takes to find happiness. If you truly love someone, then what makes them happy makes you happy too. It's not about owning each other. It's about being close friends with each other, being honest with each other, even when it hurts to be honest.

A NEW CHAPTER

2015

Finally, the day of my first speaking event dawned. As Nick drove to the University of Melbourne, I repeated the opening lines of my speech to myself over and over again.

In this world we live in, many things will happen to us that are… I knew if I got the introductory lines right, I'd be able to confidently take it from there. The rest of my talk would be about my story, my life and the journey that had brought me to this moment.

I arrived at the venue brimming with enthusiasm, all excited about addressing a large gathering. When I glanced into the hall, however, I found just a small group there. What am I doing here? I thought, but immediately quelled the feeling of disappointment rising in me. It didn't matter if I'd be addressing a small gathering. Everyone has to start somewhere, I told myself. This was going to be a great learning experience. If I was going to make mistakes in my first appearance, it was better to do it in front of a small crowd, rather than a large one.

I began to practise my opening lines in my head. In this world we live in, many things… Just then, Poni, the MC for the conference, walked in, throwing a big smile at me. She had smiles and hugs for the audio team and everyone backstage. We chatted for a while, and when I confided in her that I was feeling a bit nervous, she said, 'Liza, you're here to do a job. You're doing what you were meant to do, so just do it.'

Her words of encouragement instantly put me at ease. With a few minutes to go before I went on stage, I took a peek at the few dozen people seated around dinner tables in the auditorium. Among the audience were important people from different communities around Australia and even some who'd travelled from Africa.

Poni was already out there, addressing the audience. One more minute and then I would have to step on stage. My stomach felt tied in a knot and my heart pounded in my chest.

I heard Poni say to the crowd, 'I met a beautiful lady this evening, and she said to me, "I want to be the next Oprah Winfrey". Then I heard her story and you know what? She has all that it takes to be the next Oprah Winfrey. So here she is, ladies and gentlemen. Please join me in welcoming Liza Pavlakos.'

I was taken by surprise when Poni disclosed my secret wish to the audience. She'd given me a superb introduction. It was now up to me to deliver the goods. I walked onto the stage to the sound of enthusiastic clapping. On reaching the middle of the stage, I greeted the audience and, after a brief hesitation, tried to open with the lines I'd been practising for several days.

'In this world we live in, many things will… In this world we live in, many things… er…' I was so embarrassed about fumbling the words that my mind went blank.

I stood there silently with the microphone in my hand and scanned the faces of the people in the audience, all watching me and waiting.

I was getting more desperate with every passing second. I closed my eyes briefly and then looked at the audience again with fresh eyes, this time as a group of people in need of my help and started my talk again.

'I'm so sorry. I'd practised what I was going to say, but for some reason, I can't remember the exact words. I guess I'm too nervous. However, I'm not going to let that stop me from talking to you.'

Before I knew it, I began telling them my story, the childhood abuse, running away from home, attempting suicide, being battered by an abusive husband. I revealed the hell I'd been through, but I kept the narration concise, without making it melodramatic in any way. I didn't want my talk to be depressing. Then, I quickly moved on to my achievements: my first Miss India International show, my business successes. It was important to me that the resilience that pulled me out of misery made a greater impact on my audience than the pain inflicted on me. I wanted to show them how I'd resolutely gone from beaten and battered to self-confident and successful.

I ended by stressing the importance of believing in ourselves no matter if everyone, including those closest to us, failed to stand by us. We had to take the responsibility for transforming our own lives. Every obstacle needed to be looked at as a challenge, as something that could be overcome through tenacity and courage. Adversities might knock us down, but resilience would help us bounce back and move forward.

'My own life is an example,' I told them. 'You have just one life. I urge you to live it to the fullest.'

When I finished, from the applause that seemed to go on and on, I grasped my talk had been well appreciated. I went straight to Nick for his reaction. I was grateful that he'd come to support me. It was the middle of the Spring Racing Carnival, one of the busiest times of the year for our tailoring stores, but he was there by my side, taking photos and watching me speak.

'So, how was it?' I said happily.

Nick said, 'I don't know. It seemed good. Anyway, this was your first talk. I guess you'll only get better.'

It wasn't exactly what I'd been hoping to hear. Nick hadn't said I was terrible. But he hadn't said my talk was great either. Then Poni came up to me and said, 'Liza, you were fantastic!'

Another woman, Marion, said, 'Let me give you a hug and tell you how awesome you are.'

She led me to a crowd of women standing in line waiting to meet me. Many shook my hand and told me how much they'd enjoyed listening to me. Others wanted their photos taken with me, and some even asked for my autograph.

The experience was simply amazing. I told myself that perhaps I'd just gotten a taste of what was to come. That day, I also learned my first lesson as a motivational speaker. It doesn't matter if you practise your speech a few times or a thousand times. When you speak from the heart, people will listen.

By the time we got home, I realised why Nick wasn't too fulsome in his praise of my talk. He wanted me to shine as an even better speaker. I went to bed that night delighted I'd taken my first step and a confident one at that, into the world of motivational speaking.

MAKING PEACE WITH MY PARENTS

2016

My relationship with Nick wasn't the only one that was evolving as I transformed my thinking and healed. Late one evening, Daddy surprised me by inviting us to have dinner with Norida and him at their house the following Sunday. Prior to this, he'd never suggested that I meet or interact with Norida in any way.

Also, despite his split from Mummy and the conflicts over his ongoing relationship with Norida, he'd never said bad things about Mummy to me. Not even when I'd requested him to urgently step in and look after my children while Nick and I were in the Maldives. And he didn't take advantage of the situation to provoke a rift between me and Mummy either. Instead, when I was annoyed with her decision to return to Malaysia, he'd tried to calm me down.

So, when he asked us to dinner, I didn't feel he was exploiting the rough patch that my relationship with Mummy was going through to get me to accept Norida. I accepted his invite and said that all of us—Nick, the children, and I—would come.

Daddy said, 'Are you sure, Liza? This could upset your mother.'

Of course it would upset her. Over the years, I'd seen how she reacted when she felt people had betrayed her by talking to

Norida or having her in their house. I was scared of betraying her, but the more I worked on healing myself, loving myself, I realised it wasn't about Mummy; it was about me. I had to do what was right for me.

'Yes, I know that,' I said, trying to reassure Daddy. 'But I think it's time I visited you and Norida. I need to do this.'

My entire life, I'd always had this idea in my head that when Daddy died, I'd arrive at his funeral and scream my head off at her, tell her she was selfish, that she had broken up my family and that I hated her for ruining my parents' life and my own. Now that I was older, I knew I had to consider both sides of the whole unpleasant situation. I couldn't disregard the loyalty I'd always felt toward my mother, but I couldn't help admitting that perhaps my anger toward Norida was misplaced and it was my father who'd chosen to transfer his parental responsibilities to our mother. I was sad for Mummy and how it had ended for her and I wished I could convince her that what had happened was for the best. What was the point in being with a man if he didn't love you, the way you deserved to be loved?

That Sunday, as we drove to Daddy's place, the thought that my mother might consider this visit a betrayal was never far from my mind. Daddy, Norida and my half-brother and his wife all stepped outside to greet us while we were parking the car. As we entered the house, Daddy placed a little sugar in our mouths; he was blessing us in the traditional way. This was symbolic of how much it meant to him that we were visiting their house for the first time.

Norida greeted us with a polite hello. I suspected she was nervous too. The house was clean, simple and organised. But that was very much in line with Daddy's nature. He preferred a simple lifestyle to extravagance.

Before dinner was served, Nick and Daddy chatted and my

half-brother and his wife played with the children; I was happy to sit back and just observe this family that had never been a part of my life yet had played a huge part in it.

I appreciated that Norida didn't impose herself on the children. She looked delighted to meet them yet didn't ask them to call her grandma or chat with her. She just let them be. The kitchen table could seat only four or five of us. And so, Daddy, Nick, my two youngest daughters, and I were asked to dine there. Norida served dinner and then sat on the lounge with my half-brother, his wife and the rest of the children.

Although dinner went smoothly, I was relieved to get out of there. I needed time to process what was happening. I had to get over my long-standing hostility toward Norida and to show Daddy I'd forgiven him for moving on. However, I also realised my frustration was not really about him walking out of his marriage but about how he still continued to be close to my uncle who'd sexually abused me. Once, when I asked my father why he'd never stood up for me, his answer was, 'Liza, it's not that I don't believe you. But as you know, in Islam, we don't have the right to judge others.'

I had to admit I couldn't judge my father for what he chose to believe or do either; I had to simply acknowledge I didn't agree with him. And if I resented anything, it was the choice he and Norida made to accept a paedophile, who has never asked for forgiveness nor been punished for what he did, into their life. Nonetheless, I still valued our relationship. But I had to also be prepared to deal with the possibility of Mummy thinking I'd betrayed her and, at the same time, I had to accept I badly needed to find closure for myself. Pondering over all this as we continued driving home, it felt like I was battling my mother's and father's demons as well as my own, all at once.

My venturing into keynote speaking was helping me recognise the demons in my life that were restraining me from healing and moving forward. It brought home to me the bitter truth that if I was to help others, I needed to first start practising what I intended to preach.

I spent a lot of time after that dinner at Daddy's house, thinking about his relationship with Mummy and Norida. For years, Mummy had loved Daddy and fought to keep him with her even though she knew he was still seeing Norida. On the other hand, Norida had spent most of her life with Daddy behind closed doors. She was always the other woman who'd waited on the sidelines and remained loyal for years, because she loved him so much. The problems in my own marriage helped me see that nothing in life could be labelled as fully black or fully white. Relationships, especially matters of the heart, were too complicated to be analysed simplistically.

A few weeks later, Daddy stopped by one afternoon to visit the kids. He'd brought Norida with him. I realised this could be the opportunity to gain closure to the earlier, painful "Norida chapter" of my life. As they stepped across the threshold of my house, I knew I would never scream at Norida at Daddy's funeral. I didn't hate her anymore. Besides, I now also accepted Daddy's life was his life and not mine to control. I only wished he'd handled things with Mummy better and had the courage to opt out of his marriage to her much earlier. Another unfulfilled wish I'd held onto was that he would have the decency and kindness to apologise to my mother for the emotional abuse he put her through across the lifetime of their marriage.

I left Daddy playing with the kids and then Norida and I had a little chat in the kitchen out of earshot of the others. I came clean with her about hating her in the past and now appreciating all she was doing to keep Daddy happy and support his need to nurture his bond with me and my siblings and his grandchildren as well.

I told her, 'My mother suffered tremendously because of your affair with Daddy. And I know you suffered as well, always being labelled as the other woman your entire life with him. But then, I've suffered too because of you and my father choosing to maintain a relationship with my uncle who betrayed my trust in him by doing things to my body that no child should have to endure. Everyone deserves justice for their suffering. If I have one wish, therefore, it is that he should be reprimanded for his actions. But I can't control your choices. What I can do is tell you that for any hurt I have caused you, I am sorry. Just the same, I wish you would give my mother the respect and justice she deserves. It would be nice if one day you make peace with her.'

Norida listened quietly as I got it all off my chest. When I finished, she hugged me and said, 'I'm really sorry for the pain you and your mother had to endure. But I never wanted to hurt anybody.'

Daddy walked in, and we hastily ended our conversation, saying, 'God knows best.'

For individuals committed to their faith, this line says so much in just three short words. By believing that God knows everything, our every thought and intention, no matter how much we believe we aren't responsible for our actions or words, we are always accountable.

We are the ones who are in control and when we grow and mature, emotionally and psychologically, we have the power to make the right decisions, provided we have built the right foundations of understanding, insight and self-belief.

Now that I'd started the process of identifying, confronting and vanquishing my inner demons, I knew I would soon have to deal with perhaps the greatest of them all – my anguished relationship with my mother. It would be the toughest one to tackle because we'd been so close over the years. Being too close also meant it was much easier for us to hurt each other. Whenever she failed to show the courage to stand up for me, it would make me feel worthless and dejected. Now, I realise she herself was voiceless. She was a victim of Daddy's emotional abuse, as well as the abuse she suffered as a child.

As a youngster, I used to make excuses for her lack of support toward me. She didn't have the strength to defy Daddy, other relatives, and society, I'd tell myself. But now I had children of my own, I was fully aware of the extent to which I would go to stand by them and their goals in life. I also knew all about how a mother should never treat her children and that she should never give anything more importance than their well-being.

Even when Mummy didn't seem too enthused about me telling my story for the benefit of others or pursuing a speaking career, I believed it was because she thought I should just stick with the tailoring business that was doing really well and keeping me financially stable. I knew, having suffered a lot of pain herself, she hated that my goal of becoming a speaker would be achieved at the cost of having to relive the horrors of my past and reopen old wounds on stage, over and over again. But most of all, I knew she was hurting because of the shame of not protecting me the way she could or should have in the past. But now I didn't want "should have" or "could have" to figure in our communications with each other, because now is all we have. And neither did I want to hold on to the pain of my mother's failure to protect me as a child any longer.

I missed the close relationship I enjoyed with Mummy while she lived in Australia. I was sure my children were missing her too. So, I decided to take my daughters Alyana, Azahra and Amira with me and fly home to Malaysia for a month. Mummy knew we were coming, though she didn't know exactly when. Our arrival time being late at night, I'd arranged for one of my cousins to pick us up at the airport and take us to Mummy's house.

It was midnight when Alyana reached up and rang her doorbell. I thought Mummy looked frail as she peered warily through the window at us. When she recognised who was outside her door that late at night, she yelled, 'Lizaaaaa!'

The joy in Mummy's voice and on her face melted my heart. Once we were inside and were done with a whole lot of hugging, I went to bed that night feeling happy I'd decided to visit her. Shortly before visiting Mummy, I'd been invited to talk as a motivational speaker for an African radio show. I'd emailed links to the few episodes I'd done until then, to a number of people, including Mummy. She had an iPhone and an Apple computer, the devices that I too used for listening to my radio talk show, but she always said she wasn't able to open the files. That was so disappointing, as I was eager for her to listen to them.

I was delighted that another episode of the radio show was about to be broadcast while I was there with her and I asked Mummy to listen to it along with me.

'Why don't you go to your room and listen to it, Liza?' she said. 'That way, you can listen without any interruption.'

I felt hurt that she didn't want to listen to my show with me.

'Why don't you support me in what I'm doing?' I said.

She didn't answer my questions. Instead, she said, 'Okay, okay, I'll listen to it.'

But that wasn't how I wanted it to be. How could I be happy about her listening to me talk when I knew she was only doing it to appease me?

'No, you don't have to,' I said to her. 'I know you don't give a shit about my talk.'

'Liza, don't be angry. Come on, let's listen to it.'

Unfortunately, by the time I put the radio show on, we'd already missed the first segment. Still, I was glad she got to hear me talk about how I felt when she had cancer and how much I loved her.

When the episode ended, she said, 'That was beautiful. I can't believe that you are speaking. Why do you worry about what other people think of you, when you can speak so well and can offer such good advice? You should take your own advice and believe in yourself.'

I don't know if she realised this or not, but her answer disgusted me. On the one hand, she seemed really impressed with my show; on the other, she'd said something demeaning. Why couldn't she have said something like, 'Liza, you speak so well and you're doing a good thing helping others' and leave it at that instead of turning the conversation to me not practising what I preached and worrying about what others thought?

Besides, I wasn't the one anxious about what others thought. Yes, I did worry about what she and Daddy thought and about making them proud of me. But that was when I was much younger. I had watched my parents always worrying about "society's" perception of their image and what people thought of them, concerns that seemed more important to them than their responsibility to stand up for me against the family members who had hurt me so badly. For almost my entire life, instead of protecting my interests, my parents were always sweeping anything negative, hurtful or embarrassing concerning me under the carpet so people wouldn't think badly of them.

I remembered another time I'd sent Mummy the link to

one of my short YouTube videos, titled Good Thoughts. It was a clipping of me encouraging people to think positively if they wanted to lead better lives. The next day I called her to ask what she thought of it.

'Oh, it was okay,' she'd said. And then she added, mimicking my voice, 'You need to have good thoughts.'

Though it hurt that she was making a joke of my video, I didn't make any comment, choosing to ignore the way she'd responded and her lack of support or appreciation. I haven't watched that video again.

I was slowly beginning to realise Mummy would never support my desire to make a career in motivational speaking. So, I deliberately pushed aside my disappointment and focused on enjoying the rest of my time in Malaysia with her.

One evening, I left the girls with her and spent the day out with my favourite Uncle Apali, who was my mother's youngest brother and someone who had always been so kind and loving to me. I often looked at him as if he was my father. Uncle Apali meant the world to me, so spending time with him was always the highlight. This particular uncle has such a caring and nurturing nature and, because I knew he would never bring harm to me, I felt safe and secure in his presence. When I returned, I found my cousins Sahida and June there with her.

Sahida said, 'Well, it looks like your baby doesn't have any problem with Maleek. She went to his housewarming party.'

I was stunned. I knew about my cousin's party but had no intention of attending it. And I certainly didn't think anyone would take my children to it, considering they all knew how I felt about Maleek.

'No. Amira didn't go to that party,' I said.

'Yes, she did,' Sahida said, smiling at me. 'June took her.'

'Is this true?' I said, turning to June, shocked that anyone would do such a thing behind my back.

'Yes, it's true, and why are you making a big deal about it?' June said.

'Why a big deal? Because Maleek raped me when I was a teenager and I don't want him anywhere near my children. How did you dare to take my child to his house?' I couldn't believe it. I'd thought my children would've been safe with my mother.

When my cousins left, I exploded, 'Mummy! How could you allow my child to go to a rapist's house? How could you do this to me?'

'Believe me, Liza, I didn't want to let June take Amira because I knew you wouldn't like it. I said "no" a few times, but she insisted. She felt she was helping by taking care of Amira.'

The emotions coursing inside me spun and twisted into a fireball of rage.

'I hate you! I fucking hate you!' I shouted at her.

'Okay, fine. It's all my fault,' she yelled back at me.

'But how could you hurt me when I love you so much, Mummy? What if that rapist had hurt my baby?'

'Well, I'm a horrible mother. I'm... I'm just useless. What about you?' Mummy practically spat the words at me. 'How could you allow that bitch, Norida, to come to your house?'

I couldn't believe she'd turned an argument about her letting my little daughter go to the home of one of my abusers into an argument about the woman my father had an affair with.

'Mummy, why are you equating Daddy's affair with the seriousness of rape and sexual abuse? While affairs are wrong, those who commit sexual crimes should face legal consequences. In Malaysia, under Sharia law, someone who sexually assaults or forces another person against their will can be imprisoned for up to 15 years and fined!'

Mummy thumped her chest with her right hand and her eyes bulged.

'She did more than rape me,' she yelled. 'She took my husband. She took my whole life away from me. She stripped me of my dignity.'

I looked at Mummy and thought, I'm not buying this anymore. She needs to accept the truth.

'No,' I said firmly, 'she didn't take anything away from you. You left Daddy because he didn't deserve you. But why are you making this conversation about them, when it's about you betraying me?'

I could see that even after so many years, Mummy still wasn't ready to let go of her pain and anger. I wondered how much of that anger was directed at Norida and Daddy and how much of it was directed at herself for not leaving Daddy sooner.

For a brief moment, I mulled over trying to make her see sense.

Marriage can be challenging as people evolve. If your partner has an affair, it's not your fault but a result of their own issues. Affairs are harmful distractions and responses vary – some forgive, others part ways. Remember, no one can break you but yourself. The choice is yours: harbour bitterness or take control to forgive, heal and find true happiness in pursuing your dreams.

I wish I could share all of this with Mum.

I was too exhausted to explain anything to her. Also, the thought of my daughter being in Maleek's house had brought on feelings of intense depression. All I could think of was having the courage to fly back home in the morning. That night, I cried myself to sleep.

In the morning, I checked on my children, who were still sleeping and went to my mother's bedroom. I found her fast asleep. I just stood by her bed and stared at her sleeping form. She was so beautiful. She was my everything and I still loved her so much.

I sat on her bed and placed a hand on her shoulder.

'Mummy. Wake up, Mummy,' I said.

She came awake slowly. 'Liza? What's wrong?'

'I have to leave. I don't want to, but I have to go.'

She sat up, eyes still heavy with sleep.

'You're going because you don't love me.'

'I do love you, Mummy. It's just that... forget it.'

She said, 'Sahida said she's sorry. I spoke to everyone. They're all sorry.'

'Really? And I should be grateful they're sorry?'

'They really are sorry, Liza. Just stay. Don't worry about anything.'

My heart was breaking as we spoke. Mummy was once again implying I needed to put up with all the horrible things my cousins had said and done to me.

'I'm so sorry, Mummy. You should never have allowed my child to go to that house. It's not about telling June, "Liza won't like it." It's about you actually saying, "This is my beloved grandchild. I will not allow anyone who has abused my precious daughter to be anywhere around her or her child." I'm sorry, I can't stay.'

The phone rang. It was Sahida. I heard Mummy saying into the phone, 'She's leaving. Yes, please do come. This has to end, once and for all.'

When Sahida arrived, I walked down the stairs in my silk kaftan.

'Akka, sister,' I said, 'this has nothing to do with you. It's between me and my mum.'

She wasn't interested in listening to me. Instead, she pleaded with me to see her view.

'Why, Liza? Why all the drama? Maleek is leading a happy married life. Why do you want to disturb the peace? Honestly, everyone has been hurt enough already. Now forget everything and just get on with your life, Liza.'

I looked at her with a cold indifference.

'I don't have to justify anything to you. I've nothing to say to you.'

She said, 'One day you'll regret this. You'll regret not listening to me and beg my forgiveness. And one day your mother will die and then you'll admit your mistake and ask for forgiveness for what you've done.'

I was shocked.

'What have I done? How can you blame it all on me? This isn't just about what your brother did. It's about everything that happened after that as well. It's about running away because I didn't feel safe at home, about being forced into a marriage with an abusive husband, about having my face broken, about being abducted and almost murdered. It's about attempting suicide, my severe depression, do you have any idea what happens to a person when they go through all of that? Tell me you understand what that is like! Tell me!' I was screaming by the time I finished.

Mummy and Sahida ignored my shouting completely, as if they were deaf and blind.

I went upstairs to find my children were now awake. They'd heard all the commotion downstairs.

A short while later, we left, and I cried all the way to the hotel.

I felt at ease staying in the Ritz Carlton in Kuala Lumpur. It was like a second home to me. Surprisingly, my mother didn't seem interested in visiting me or her own grandchildren during this time. The only person who came to see me was her sister, Auntie Begum. My relationship with Auntie Begum had been a bit distant, but I always admired her. Her husband passed away when her children were young and she did everything to protect them from harm. I often wished she could be my mother because she was so protective. She kept her home perfectly tidy and she had a fantastic sense of style. She was someone I really looked up to.

When Auntie Begum visited, she brought each of my three daughters a doll as a lovely gift. She took us for walks and spent quality time with us. Auntie Begum tried to give me advice, encouraging me to stand up for myself and let go of the family that had hurt me. But emotionally, I was too fragile at that point to fully grasp what I needed to do for myself. I pretended I wanted to be independent, but deep down, I wasn't ready to cut ties with anyone. I wanted to be a part of my whole family, including my cousins and I wished they would support me. I knew they wouldn't tolerate this kind of treatment if it happened to their own children, but I was expected to endure this deep betrayal and unfairness.

I returned home to Melbourne carrying a deep sadness in my heart. In the days that followed, I often found myself thinking, if only Mummy and I could put our love first, put our love above everything else and stop hurting each other. If only Mummy had been firm and prevented June from taking Amira.

Nevertheless, I was proud of one thing. I'd walked away from Mummy, badly hurt but without hating her. I still loved her.

Today, I've no problem admitting my mother might never

be exactly how I want her to be and I might not be the Liza that, deep in her heart, Mummy wants me to be. But I know that's okay. Because with realisation like that, comes acceptance.

I wished my mother knew what Maleek did to me and how, the fact his family condoned his actions, was not only a grievous offence to me, but to her as well. No mother should endure the pain of her daughter being abused and I feel sorry for her, that my mother did not know how to deal with the emotional fallout it created. The only way to deal with it, from her perspective, was to not deal with it at all.

My mother always dealt with things differently from me. She was raised in a different time and era. I understood her pain and trauma, and I believe that maybe she didn't know how to accept or deal with the things her only daughter had to go through. Perhaps, I was the one who needed to learn to be more compassionate. Perhaps, I had to learn to give up having expectations from others.

In my heart, I know who my mother is and love her deeply. And even though she might not have believed in me sometimes, I will always believe in her. My parents are old. I don't have the power to keep them in my life for as long as I want to. But I can control the kind of feelings I have for them. Here I'm reminded of what my favourite poet Rumi wrote:

Life asked death, why do people love me, but hate you? Death responded, it's because you're a beautiful lie and I'm the painful truth.

So, if life is short and death is inevitable for all of us, how can I continue to harbour anger toward my parents?

Today, whenever the thought of anyone who has physically and emotionally hurt me creeps into my mind, I wish they feel sorry for what they did to me and never hurt anybody else. They mean nothing to me. Also, I no longer feel I have to justify to anyone why I am who I am. Or justify the choices I make.

Now, I no longer believe real happiness comes from branded products or a luxurious lifestyle. I may buy something expensive if I like it. Not to impress others or because I believe contentment comes from owning such things. Now all I want is to find inner peace. I want to be happy, living in the present moment. I realise I'm not a terrorised victim anymore and I have the power to change the narrative of my life. Now, I realise I can't change the way people think, I can't make them accept the things I want them to accept.

Perhaps it's not that my father doesn't love me. It's just that he doesn't know how to love himself. For if he loved himself, he would realise his daughter being hurt is actually a part of him, a part of his soul and he might actually feel the pain.

Have I ever wondered how difficult it was for my brothers when I left home? Did I wonder what it was like for my half-brother, who grew up in a home where he wasn't able to grow up without me and his brothers as his loving, connected siblings?

And what about my extended family? How has this affected them? Perhaps they did not know how to handle the situation, nor did they want to be a part of it.

When it comes to Nick's family, perhaps they just wanted to protect him. They might have wanted an uncomplicated marriage for him, as marrying a woman with a history of trauma, is going to come with its own difficulties.

No one is bad or wrong in these cases. Each individual in the world just views it through their own unique lens and those lenses might not align with yours or mine.

I can't control anyone, but I can choose to love, to live, to forgive and that is what this book is about.

Perhaps spending time to reflect on other people's perspective, believing there is no wrong and no right, is the civilised way to exist together. This is life. It's an endless journey of triumphs and tribulations and the only journey we can focus on with clarity and any real form of control, is cultivating our spirituality to guide us through life, with all its beauty and pitfalls. Like fine red wine, we all age in time and become mature and with time we reflect and make better choices.

Having found this peace within myself, I feel like I'm the wealthiest person on earth and I continue to change the narrative of my life with pure positivity. It's possible and it's worth it.

You are worth it.

PEOPLE, PASSION AND PUTTING MY LIFE AT RISK

2017

No job is ever completely undemanding. Mine has stress-related elements too. While there have been so many exhilarating moments – moments when I have had an audience of 4000 people rise to their feet and applaud my talk, times when women have approached me after a keynote address and told me, with tears in their eyes, how sharing my story has given them the strength they need to shift away from their own dangerous situations and times when hundreds of people have queued to meet me, shake my hand, get an autograph or take a photo with me – there are times when the emotional and mental drain becomes incredibly exhausting. No matter how fatigued I am at the end of a presentation, though, those interactions I have with people, who share something of themselves with me and thank me for sharing so much of my own life, always manage to re-energise and motivate me.

The insights my travels gave me were invaluable. Yes, some elements were definitely confronting but every moment was also an experience to understand the world around me better – as well as understand myself.

By the time I touched down in Manila, to head to my main event on my second official speaking engagement and my first international invitation, I was overwhelmed by the fearful thought that I was all on my own in a foreign country. A symptom of my own PTSD is a tendency to look over my shoulder repeatedly when I am in strange places.

What if something happened to me while I was far away from my family?

What if I got into a bad car accident?

These kinds of frightful thoughts raced through my mind and were hard to stop. But when it was time for me to fly home, I left with a heart bursting with joy. And with gratitude. I realised the miseries I'd endured in the past had given me some positive traits, including the ability to empathise with others who'd gone through their own traumatic life experiences. My sufferings had made me a more genuine motivational speaker. If I'd given into my fears and doubts when I arrived, I never would have experienced those insights and benefits.

On that same speaking tour to the Philippines, I visited the Our Lady of Perpetual Help Children's Home. The visit was both poignant and heartening. I learned about the selfless services of the good sisters and their dedication to caring for orphaned children and felt a genuine sense of satisfaction. It made me realise the full significance of what I was doing. I wasn't spending my day helping parentless children like those nuns, so I am not comparing my public speaking engagements with what they do, but I was, in my own way, helping people overcome serious challenges in their lives.

The following year, in 2017, I had the privilege of being invited to speak at the Spark Up Leadership Conference at Benin City, Nigeria, a short distance from Lagos. That trip is also etched in my memory, but because of something I'd rather forget.

I was travelling with my cameraman, Matt, as well as my

former nanny, now my assistant, Rosie, and had to deal with a boring 24-hour stopover in the Middle East. We decided to book a local driver to take in some sightseeing to pass the time.

Truth be told, I wasn't keen on going sightseeing and would've preferred to spend the day in the hotel. But because I wanted to be a team player and Matt and Rosie were so keen to explore the city, I decided to tag along. Besides, it wasn't as if I'd be travelling through the Middle East regularly and because I wasn't going out alone, there was no reason to feel unsafe.

Our driver seemed like a friendly kind of guy and was happy to make as many stops as we liked to check out the mall, the markets and some other interesting places. Each time we got out, he would remind us to leave our shopping bags in the vehicle instead of lugging them around, assuring us there was no risk in leaving them there. We'd heard the city was absolutely safe, like Singapore, so we were only too glad to take his advice.

A little later, when the driver suggested we take a tour of the magnificent landscapes of the nearby desert, we gladly agreed to do that as well. But as he drove us toward the isolated expanse, I had a gut feeling that everything was not okay. I didn't say anything to the others. I didn't want to seem paranoid or ungrateful. After all, we knew Uber tracks the movements of its drivers. What we didn't know, however, was that unscrupulous drivers know ways to override the company's tracking mechanism.

When we boarded the plane in Melbourne, I noticed Matt had a drone with him and wondered why he'd brought it along on this trip. I was even more surprised when, even though we had not yet reached the desert and were still in the heart of the city, Matt asked our driver if he could fly it to capture aerial shots of the place. Especially since he didn't seem to be acquainted with the rules of the land regarding such devices. What we did not predict was, what seemed like a careless move on his part proved to be the lifeline we needed to survive an extremely dangerous situation.

Several things happened next, suddenly and in rapid succession. Within a few minutes of Matt flying the drone, we were surrounded by police vehicles and military investigators. I managed to make a quick call to Nick but barely had time to tell him we were being detained and where we were, before our passports and mobile phones were confiscated for thorough checking and the four of us, including our driver, were taken into custody. People who identified themselves as police, some in uniform, some in plainclothes, bundled Matt into one car and Rosie and me into another.

I was terrified, wondering what was about to happen. In some foreign countries, getting detained by police can have disastrous consequences. And who knew where we were? Or where we were going? In that moment of feeling out of control for my own safety, my first response was to freeze in silent panic. My mind, though, was racing through a series of thoughts and possible outcomes, each one worse than the last. I wanted to scream but my voice had no sound. I wanted to jump out of the car but knew I had nowhere to run to.

My mind flew back to the time when I sat in the kidnapper's car, a scared-stiff 19-year-old, not knowing where I was being taken. And just like then, I couldn't make sense of what was happening to me. Was this just a bad dream? I wondered when it would end and free me from the panic rising up inside me.

Why had I even come on this trip? I wondered when I would see my children again.

We were driven to some military establishment and spent the next 16 hours or so in confinement, racked with fear. Rosie and I were put into the women's cell and Matt into the men's. Before that, our phones and passports hadn't been returned to us and we were subjected to intense investigation.

We learned that Matt faced the threat of being charged with espionage for flying a drone in the Middle East and Rosie and I, with being his accomplices. We were shit-scared of being suspected smugglers or terrorists and incarcerated inside a jail, miles away from home and family, for God knew how long.

I sat on the floor in the cell, petrified into silence. A woman warden was keeping watch over us, a deadpan expression on her face. I wondered if she might empathise with me if I explained my plight to her.

Asking her if she could bring me a prayer mat helped on two counts. First, it could help me build a rapport with her. Second, it would actually help me pray in silence. Anything to ease my worries and escape the dark thoughts starting to close in on me.

When I was kidnapped, all those years earlier, it was only me in that dangerous situation and, ultimately, only me who could get myself out of it.

This time, I was responsible for the safety and well-being of Matt and Rosie as well.

Poor Rosie. I could see the fright reflected in her eyes. But all I could do was look back at her and convey a silent message of reassurance.

I began to pray in earnest. Indeed, there wasn't a prayer that I didn't pray that day. Around two hours after handing me a prayer mat, the warden finally said something to me.

'What do you do?' she said, in broken English.

I perked up immediately. This was my moment to try and win her over to my side. I asked if she had a phone. She did. I said I wanted to go to YouTube. She nodded and handed me her phone. Everything was in Arabic. Realising this, she took the phone back, changed the keyboard to English, and returned it to me.

I typed, 'Liza Pavlakos' into YouTube and a long list of videos about me showed up. I picked the one from CNN and showed it to the warden.

Her eyes widened. 'Famous?'

'Yes,' I said. 'I help underprivileged girls. Traumatised women. I help people. Could you please help me?'

I hoped that seeing the CNN video, in which I was featured as a thought leader from Australia, would plant the seed in her mind that I was someone important and, if I was detained, it would eventually make world news.

The moment she finished watching the video, I bowed down at her feet and clung to them with both hands as I broke down and begged for freedom.

'I haven't done anything wrong,' I said. 'I've five young children. Please help me.'

All I got from the warden was a helpless look. But my pleas must have had an impact because a military official strode into the cell a few minutes later. My team and I had narrowly escaped being trafficked or murdered, he told me. They'd found out our driver was a human trafficker and had plans of abducting us. I listened to him in horror, unable to say a word.

Later, we found out the investigations carried out by the military had thrown up some startlingly horrific information about our driver. He turned out to be a cold-blooded human-trafficking agent. They found his mobile phone had a secret gallery with hundreds of images and videos of his unfortunate victims. There were pictures of young girls and women, tied up and gagged, their faces marked by gruesome bruises, pictures of men being shot and of women being bound and raped.

When we were finally set free, almost 17 hours after being detained, we were given bland, stale rice with scraps of meat, as well as a small amount of water as our only sustenance. Even Rosie, who was vegan, ate the meat in her desperate hunger, but for me, PTSD had set in and I had no appetite.

Finally, we were released and could board our flight to Lagos in time. When they dropped us off, the police reminded us how lucky we were to come out of that desert unharmed and alive. They also told us we had the option of flying back home, all the way to Australia. To be honest, I was sorely tempted to forget all about the conference and get onto the first flight to Melbourne. But a part of me didn't want to give up. Deep inside my heart, I knew if I did, I would be left with only terrifying memories of what had just happened. Conversely, if I went ahead and spoke at the conference, the experience of interacting with women in need of support would overturn the trauma I'd just been through and even help me heal.

Suddenly, Matt's presence that day felt like some sort of guardian angel in my life. What if Matt hadn't packed a drone along with his stuff for the trip? And what if he hadn't thought of using it in that desert? Imagining what could have happened: human trafficking, torture, perhaps death or a brutal lifetime of sexual slavery. It distressed me so much, I felt like I couldn't breathe. The terror of human trafficking hit me harder than ever before. At that moment, I made up my mind to be more actively involved in spreading awareness about this despicable crime that had come so close to changing my life forever.

Yet again, I realised, whatever we have to go through in life teaches us something, so we can learn from the experience. The choice to recognise the learning and understand the lesson though, is ours.

In my case, I could either choose to look at myself as an unfortunate victim or consider that I had, instead, been gifted the opportunity to learn more life lessons that would help me become an even better, more authentic mentor to traumatised women and others crushed by adversities.

From that day, I decided as I went about my work, whether in my home country or abroad, I would be guided by this purpose and save the energy for that, rather than endlessly worrying about my personal safety and what might possibly go wrong.

That experience had badly shaken all three of us, but it didn't stop us from taking up our responsibilities the moment we got to Benin City. I was determined to step on stage for my talk without letting anyone catch the slightest hint of what we'd endured just a few hours earlier.

A few months later, in 2018, I flew to New York to speak at the WIN Summit, once again with a stopover in that same city in the Middle East. I'd been invited to speak as a successful businesswoman who'd triumphed against all odds.

On the first leg of the journey from Melbourne, I got chatting with the air hostess at the bar in business class. She told me her name was Karisma and asked what I did. I was a motivational speaker, I told her, on my way to an event. Then, for some inexplicable reason, I began to tell Karisma all about my life. She listened to me in silence. After a brief pause, she startled me by saying she'd been raped too. She was just five years old when she was gang-raped by four men. It broke my heart to hear this. I could feel that lovely girl's pain. We met as strangers and, in an instant, we connected as two human beings empathising with a shared experience of anguish and shame. There were tears sparkling in her eyes, when Karisma admitted she'd just told me things she'd never told anyone else before.

'Those savages shattered my peace of mind forever,' she said.

I looked her in the eye; my voice was firm.

'You want to regain your peace of mind? Get over what those men did to you? Then use that anger bottled up inside you in a constructive way. Anger is a source of great energy. Why not take the energy from all that anger inside you and redirect it toward achieving something powerful, like your dreams? Others may hurt you. But nobody can take your dreams away from you. So don't let what those men did, stop you from fulfilling them. Don't forgive those men if you don't want to. But don't hold on to your hate either.'

'Why not? What they did to me was hateful.'

'It was. But hate is a negative force. It will weaken you. Don't get me wrong. I understand your pain. I'm just trying to make you see you're much stronger than you think. And you can get over staying fixated on those men if you make up your mind to do that.'

'But I was innocent,' she protested, her voice breaking.

'Jesus was innocent too. But see how much he had to suffer,' I said softly.

She gazed back at me for a moment, saying nothing. The next minute, we hugged each other and wept silent tears.

I went back to my seat thinking I was meant to meet this girl and touch her heart. Then I felt a twinge of worry. Had I offered her the right advice? I hoped she'd sensed the credibility in every word I'd spoken to her, that my advice had sprung from personal experience of similar painful incidents and I was being genuine when I suggested she focus on leading a rewarding life.

Yet again, I realised how, each time I offered solace and hope to someone, it made me feel that my own life was so much more meaningful.

We were nearing that stopover destination in the Middle East now and I couldn't help feeling apprehensive. But I was determined to keep my emotions in check, especially since I was alone this time. Matt was flying out to New York separately.

By the time the plane landed, I was struggling to keep calm. As I checked into the Ritz Carlton, I told myself, in the given situation, it was normal for me to feel afraid. And besides, the hotel had high security. But still I felt anxious. Feeling the panic building up inside me, I realised I needed to somehow find the strength to face my fear, no matter how justified it was.

My gut instinct was urging me.

Do something bold.

I hired a driver and drove to the same mall and markets I'd visited on the last fateful stopover. I also spent time walking down the streets on my own. By consciously repeating most of the things I'd done the last time, I was trying to rewire my brain to associate the city with this uneventful visit and disassociate all thoughts of it from feelings of fear. Even though I was as nervous as hell, I knew this was something I had to do. I didn't want anxiety to kick in each time I stopped in this beautiful Middle Eastern destination. I'd be lying if I said I didn't feel any PTSD symptoms as I was driven to the airport. What if I didn't make it there? What if I was kidnapped again?

I frantically dialled Nick's number. I sensed he too was frightened, but he managed to calm me down.

It was a long 15-hour journey from there to New York. When I finally stepped off the plane, the excitement of actually landing in NYC was overwhelming. I was thrilled about being invited to speak at an event in the US and, once I'd delivered it, it was wonderful to be so well received by the women attending the summit.

New York City is amazing and I loved every minute of my visit, but one of the happiest moments of that trip came the day after my presentation. Before leaving for the US, I'd written to an American priest I'd once befriended in the Philippines. He was delighted that I was coming to his neighbourhood and he invited me to speak at his church in Newark, the same city that was the birthplace of Whitney Houston. Barely 25 people had gathered in the small church to hear me. It was a beautiful congregation and I felt completely at ease speaking to them. The ambience was spiritual and serene and it seemed so natural, so right to slip into speaking about my own personal experiences with what I refer to as "miracles" as I delivered my motivational talk.

When I concluded my talk, the heartfelt appreciation of those people floored me. They even had a large cheque ready for me, as a special "thank you". I was deeply touched, but of course, I couldn't accept it. These good people seemed to be struggling to make ends meet, so I gave the money back to the church, because I was sure there were others in that parish more in need of the money than me.

Another uplifting experience was my second philanthropic tour in Nigeria, a little later that same year, when I had to speak at the Spark Up Leadership Conference in Benin City again. On that tour, I had the opportunity to motivate young schoolgirls to dare to dream big and strive for excellence and inspire boys at a correctional centre to shake off their fears and look toward the future with optimism and self-confidence.

The deep satisfaction of touching the hearts of young people was beyond description. Another special flow-on from that incredible experience was, I was interviewed twice on two separate popular television shows and asked to offer useful advice for the benefit of others struggling to achieve their goals.

I remember being filled with pride as I watched myself on TV sometime later while relaxing in my hotel room. It took me back to the days when, as a child, I used to watch my mother on television and how my secret desire was to be like her. Not like Janet Jackson or Beyoncé or some other international celebrity, but like my own mother. So, in a way, I fulfilled a childhood dream in Africa that year.

All the same, it was surreal watching and listening to my own televised interview. I couldn't believe I was on national TV. Was this for real? Even when I managed my four tailoring stores, it hadn't sunk in that I was a success. It didn't happen when I watched myself now on a leading television show in Nigeria either. It wasn't that I didn't believe in myself; I guess that was because I didn't consciously strive for success. I strived only to empower myself and do my best. It didn't matter if I was empowering young women through the Miss India show, my staff and customers at Finest Alterations, or the people I addressed as a keynote or motivational speaker. I just focused on doing good work. Now I was reaching millions of people via Nigerian TV. What more could I want?

My next speaking event was a philanthropic-focused gathering at a small church in Nigeria, where I was invited to address a group of around 200 young entrepreneurs. These people were so moved by my presentation and so generous with their gratitude, that they gave me two standing ovations and when I finished, the whole church prayed for me with one voice.

Oh my God... so much love! I was told the next day, the parishioners lit a special candle for me. I flew back to Melbourne after five wonderful days in Africa.

Today my connection to that amazing continent continues and I've recently become involved in a South African-based initiative that aims to stop the spread of gender-based violence. I've spoken to the organisation about setting up a Women's Information and Referral exchange that would help female victims of any kind of abuse access free advice and support and I'm proud to be given the opportunity to help improve the lives of other women and remind them that they are more than the painful reality they are caught up in at this moment.

I wish I could recount all my experiences. So many of them are memorable for one reason or another. This is how my life is now. I can't tell you how happy it makes me to help others feel confident and strong and to inspire them not to give up on their dreams.

I believe:

The sole individual you're meant to transform into is the one you choose to be.

I make sure I drive this message home to every audience I address.

MY MIND HUB: EMPOWERING MINDS

Unexpectedly, the dots will align, and you'll find your purpose waiting for you.

2019-2023

In 2019, the global pandemic hit, putting a pause on my international speaking engagements until 2023. To adapt, I quickly applied my creativity and launched Positive Breakthroughs—a counselling service aimed at helping families navigate the stress caused by the COVID pandemic. With my recent certification in running a mental health practice, I offered executive coaching and counselling, both online and in person as restrictions eased.

The success of Positive Breakthroughs fuelled my desire for more. I envisioned expanding it globally, with other coaches joining under my umbrella. However, I didn't want to use the franchise model; I needed a sustainable approach. Delving deep into my life, I found clues that led to my ultimate destiny. Reflecting on my healing journey, I recognised the vital role therapists played, from my school counsellor at 16, to a clinical psychologist at 24.

This realisation sparked the idea for My Mind Hub—a platform dedicated to providing various therapy options rooted in my own experiences. I understood that the journey to mental health is profoundly personal, shaped by each individual's unique trauma, past, growth, and mind. I chose the name My Mind Hub to emphasise that this space is not just about me, but about you—the person seeking support.

My Mind Hub serves as a central resource where individuals can explore different paths to healing and growth. It complements my speaking business, allowing me to share my message globally while offering audiences the tools they need through the My My Mind Hub of practitioners. This initiative reaffirmed my belief that true success in business lies in focusing on others, blending passion with purpose, and creating a supportive community for those navigating their own journeys.

For me, it all began with cooking, then Miss India, Piccolo Cafe, Finest Alterations and Melbourne Luxury Tailoring. This journey led me to keynote speaking, where my focus shifted towards serving others through my philanthropic organisation, the Liza Pavlakos Foundation, which ultimately led me to My Mind Hub.

Every step of the business journey we take leads us to the ultimate business plan, the ultimate idea. My Mind Hub wouldn't be possible without my personal experience of a traumatic childhood and the unique experiences I'd had as I evolved through adolescence, adulthood and motherhood.

In life, I truly believe making money is just part of the journey, however, leaving a legacy, one that makes us passionate, is what the journey is truly about.

How many people can we inspire? How many people can we influence to be better?

Whether you bake doughnuts for a living, a tailor, a carpenter, a dog walker, or a pilot, the work you do touches lives and the way you choose to do it can turn that connection into a positive impact that can help make the world a better place.

One question I always get asked by my audience after the presentation is: Who is your mentor?

Perhaps they think I'll tell them a famous name, such as Oprah Winfrey, Maya Angelou or Gabrielle Bonheur Chanel. The reality is, my mentors are my children. I have brought five kids into this world and each of them imparts distinct lessons, demonstrating how I can improve. They exhibit love, courage and the importance of perseverance, but above all, they instil in me the value of patience.

I have come to realise that not all uncles are bad, not all cousins are bad, not all people are bad. Within your circle, for every hurtful family member or friend that exists, there are good people in your corner. It's up to you to see them.

My children have each brought something unique and positive to my life. They have taught me compassion and forgiveness. They have strengthened me.

In the pond with mud, the lily flower blooms, and, just like that, you have the ability to bloom, despite your past circumstances and surroundings, because your life is precious. If we complain every step of the way, we will miss this opportunity to enjoy this world.

Today, as a motivational speaker and mentor who has walked the talk, each time I see how I can inspire and empower others to transcend obstacles, fulfil their dreams and live more rewarding lives. The satisfaction it brings me is indescribable. It makes me feel as if everything I've suffered was worth it. Which is why I truly believe I had to endure immense pain for a reason. A powerful reason.

I've seen how people wish for things to change in their life but then don't take the action that turns those wishes into achievable goals. They have dreams but do not go all out to turn them into reality. There are usually a whole lot of excuses to justify their inaction.

Where's the time?

I have so many other responsibilities.

I'm not educated enough.

I'm not rich enough.

They say losers make excuses; winners make a way. I believe that all of us are more capable and more resilient than we think we are. Those who haven't yet figured this out need to transform the way they think. In my own case, it was the way I looked at adversities that helped me break free of them. A mindset change could help you too.

Whatever your goal is – to learn to play the piano, set up your own business, go back to university for a graduate degree, become a politician, be on television, or get into social work – once you know what you want and you're passionate about achieving what you want, it's time to make a plan and create a road map for attaining it. If you can't do it on your own, consult a professional, like I did at the start of my journey and then be ready to work tirelessly and single-mindedly until you succeed. There will, almost certainly, be disappointments and roadblocks, even failure, along the way. But no matter if you stumble and fall, the ability to courageously pick yourself up each time and begin again is an incredible skill to hone. And, as they say, never, ever take your eyes off the ball. Those who are sports fans surely know what happens when a player does that. Losing focus leads to mistakes. Never get distracted from your goal, even for a moment.

Today, these are some of the key points I emphasise in my

motivational presentations. I speak on other topics too, according to the specific needs of the event organisers and the audience I am addressing, but these three topics: positive mindset change, overcoming adversities and discovering the power within, are consistently the most requested.

Motivational speaking has enabled me to live life to the fullest. Since my unassuming entry into this field in 2015, I've delivered motivational presentations across the world from Melbourne to Manila, Manhattan and Mumbai, and a number of places in between. I was, once, voiceless. Now I have regained control of my life, I use my voice to uplift others.

The joy of living my dream and knowing that what I'm doing is helping bring about positive changes in the lives of people, is something I am so grateful to experience. And in the process, in my own small way, I know I am helping change the world for the better, one person at a time.

PURPOSE, TRUST, SUCCESS AND DISCOVERY: HEALING FROM THE RAVAGES OF PTSD

I still suffer from post-traumatic stress disorder. It is a natural consequence of the immense trauma I went through in the past. I still have regular sessions with my therapist, a psychologist well-known for treating victims of crime and those who have to deal with the pressure of constantly being in the public eye. Nick and I consulted this same psychologist earlier on when we were having trouble in our marriage following the oophorectomy.

Surviving ghastly experiences and trauma is one thing. Getting over the awful memories and moving ahead is another. There was a time when my brain was constantly in fight-or-flight mode, so it was always used to thinking the worst in any situation. My therapist taught me techniques to overcome this. To combat disturbing thoughts, I had to take slow breaths and talk to my brain. I am safe. My brain, my whole body, is safe. I am in good hands. I am not alone. By repeatedly delivering positive messages to my brain, I would be rewiring my thinking brain and that would calm my nerves, my therapist told me.

If you've already read these tips on earlier pages of this book, take them seriously. Trust them. I didn't make them up, just to put words on a page. I am sharing them because they have been shared with me by someone I trust, someone with knowledge, wisdom and experience in the field of healing. And they have helped.

The counselling I continue to undertake with my therapist is a work-in-progress that has had a positive impact on my ability to deal with intrusive bad memories, as well as helping me free myself from the anger, resentment, co-dependency and other negative emotions that typically keep victims bound to their abusers.

Sometimes, the best way to heal is to let go of comparing the need for emotional and psychological healing to the healing we see when we cut our finger and wait a few days for the skin to regrow, as it was before. The scars we experience through trauma and emotional pain can become invisible, but, in lots of ways, we are forever changed. Even if we look as we always did on the outside.

Because of the ramifications of the abuse I have endured in my life, the major side-effect of that is depression. But I refuse to let such problems overshadow my determination to achieve my goals. PTSD can be debilitating, but what if I had the power to rewire my brain to think of PTSD differently?

And so, I did. For me, PTSD now stands for purpose, trust, success and discovery instead. Let me explain.

- » **Purpose.** I believe we have the power to find our purpose by listening to our inner voice and following the path that brings us true joy.
- » **Trust.** Despite my challenges, I have learned to trust my instinct and give people a chance again. Not everyone in this world is bad. You just need to trust yourself and believe in the decisions you make.
- » **Success.** It's right there within you. But triumph only comes when you believe in yourself. You need to first

believe you have the power within you to transform your life and achieve success.
» **Discovery.** Discovering your inner strength will have a positive impact on you. It will let you realise not all traumatic events will break you.

Sometimes, ordeals could help you become a stronger, more resilient version of yourself. They could help you overcome your fears and discover fearlessness. Thankfully, having ongoing treatment helps me stay resilient and strong and keep on fighting. I've changed the way I look at PTSD, but I know the emotional journey of healing still continues...

THE SIGNS ARE THERE DON'T FORGET TO LOOK

Observe the signs, follow the pebbles scattered through your life, for they guide you to your purpose.

Have you ever had a bizarre coincidence in your life and been baffled by the experience? For example, say, you have a problem to solve for which you need the right guidance from a knowledgeable person. Then one day, when you're on the bus to some place, just that kind of person takes the seat beside you, and you get talking. And you think, Wow! How did that happen? The experience says something to you that only you can perceive. You cannot explain it. But you discern that what happened has some significance, though you may not be able to grasp it completely at that moment. In religious scriptures like the Holy Bible or the Holy Quran, we read of the prophets having some strange experience or dream and recognising it as a message from Heaven.

As a spiritual person, I tend to look at amazing experiences or extraordinary coincidences that defy logical explanation, as amazing signs. Signs from a divine source communicating with my inner self to point me in the right direction. I know in the scientific age we're living in, instead of wondering about the significance of such occurrences, many may turn to the laws of probability and explain all coincidences away on the basis of science. But others, like me, may choose to reflect on them, look beneath the surface and try to discover the underlying truth.

Carl Jung considered such strange occurrences to be meaningful coincidences, which he called synchronicities. He believed synchronicities carry messages, just like dreams do, and that they take on a specific meaning based on the inner experience of an individual. For me, these aren't mere coincidences. They are meaningful signs. As I look back on my life, I realise I've had many amazing signs along the way, some of which I failed to take note of at first but then have recognised in hindsight. Let me tell you about a few of these astounding experiences that proved to be, not just emotionally but also, life-changingly significant for me.

Remember how, overcome by nerves at my first speaking event, I was mortified to find I couldn't remember the opening lines I had diligently practised? Instead of panicking, I switched to speaking spontaneously and from the heart instead, a decision that helped me make an instant connection with that small audience at the University of Melbourne. I thank my experience of running Miss India as a critical component.

Considering my dire circumstances at that time and how hopelessly vulnerable my situation was, it was nothing short of astounding that I could conceive of a daringly ambitious business idea such as planning an international event. Instead of giving in to suicidal tendencies, like I used to when gripped by feelings of dejection and frustration, I'd dared to take the plunge into something I knew nothing about. I had absolutely no experience in holding events, even for a few dozen people. So, what could have put such an idea into my head? Only years later, it dawned on me that by prompting me to hold those international pageants, a higher force that might be seen by some as subconscious, intuition, the Universe, God, or simply a heightened sense of my own potential, had laid a solid foundation for my future career as a motivational speaker.

Like it's often said, signs are everywhere. Sometimes, we may fail to recognise them and sometimes, like I've just explained, we may awaken to their significance at some later point in life.

Another sign that not everything we wish to last will be around forever is, with every door that closes, another one opens. This sign was a new beginning.

After my stint in prison in the Middle East, I moved to the Mornington Peninsula to seek a fresh start with my family in an idyllic location. This treasure of Victoria's coastline is a beautiful blend of seaside charm and rich wine country and the location provided the calm my mind needed. However, being an hour away from Nick's work created a significant problem, straining our marriage further. As time passed, we grew emotionally distant.

I yearned for more from Nick, wanting him to prioritise our family and move anywhere with us. But Nick, a workaholic committed to the family business, lost sight of me, his once-beloved wife. Perhaps from his perspective, he still considered me a priority, but deep down, I knew our problems had begun long before the move to the coast. My keynote engagements continued, and with each talk, I realised that self-love sometimes means making the toughest choices, like leaving a marriage where we no longer put each other first.

Our once-beautiful union had become mentally abusive, as we no longer understood each other. Abuse isn't always physical; it can be mental and detrimental to both partners' health.

My marriage with Nick ended and it was the most painful experience of my life. Leaving a marriage of 21 years was not easy, but in leaving, I chose to love myself against all odds.

It was a difficult time for me, but it's often in those challenging times when you realise who your real friends truly are; the ones who stand by you will stand out. One friend who fit that description perfectly was Sam.

Our children went to the same kindergarten and we were close family friends, steadfastly supporting each other through life's toughest moments. Despite Sam's divorce and my friendship with his ex-wife, our bond grew strong. He became my go-to for fixing broken cupboard doors, ferrying the kids to school during my speaking engagements, and even bringing me things I needed during hospital stays. Our relationship was built on mutual support, free from expectations or conditions.

I was caught off-guard. Sam, embodying the essence of a proper Englishman, traditional and respectful, had never blurred our friendship's boundaries. However, his quiet admiration and support led me to slowly develop feelings for him after my divorce and the sentiment was reciprocated. He didn't flinch at the fact that I was a single mother of five. Instead, he made a deliberate choice to stand by me and he honoured that decision.

Sam introduced me to his family and treated me with the respect I deserved. With him, I discovered something new within myself, the capacity to love once more and to revel in laughter. His presence brought constant joy and laughter into my life. I believe true love has the power to unlock parts of ourselves, dormant and hidden away due to lack of trust in the world. Love has a way of revealing the best aspects of who we already are but have hesitated to fully express. A dormant part of me suddenly awakened after being closed off for so long. I found myself undergoing deep emotional changes, placing a newfound value on inner peace and silence above all else.

My availability for friends changed; I became quieter and my work was no longer the centre of my attention. I still tried my best at work but was not defined by my accolades.

I asked Sam, 'Are you sure you want to be with me? I was abducted once and this comes with extreme complications. I don't take anti-depressants and I will be an emotional mess from time to time.'

Sam didn't care; he even wanted to meet with my psychologist so we could work on our relationship together with a therapist. This made me realise that no matter what, I am enough. I am worth fighting for.

Maybe Sam came into my life because I finally learned to cherish myself. These moments hinted at a greater plan – sometimes a friend becomes your life partner. The future remains uncertain, but one thing is clear: when you conquer your fears and embrace self-love, regardless of any setbacks, the unknown can surprise you.

They say the grass isn't always greener on the other side, but what if your side is barren? You must sow new seeds and embark on a fresh journey, whether with someone or alone, for yourself.

Life unfolds like a book, with chapters of both beginnings and endings.

DARE TO BE EXTRAORDINARY

As an individual, I have always been strong-willed and independent-minded. I don't like asking for permission in my personal life. I believe a marriage takes place between equals. Both partners work hard to support their family. Both partners have a right to enjoy the same freedom and the same rights.

We need to remember that no human being, not our parents, husband, sibling, friend, employer, children or anyone else, is perfect. We are all flawed. All of us have internal demons to fight. All of us have a tendency to instinctively look at things through our own personal filters. These could be our upbringing, childhood experiences, education, culture, religion or anything else. For instance, a fallout from growing up with abuse from a lover or parents, in later years, even the slightest neglect from your husband could be seen as abuse of the emotional kind. Even a mild show of irritation could be taken as a grave lack of understanding. More than other people, a person like me, therefore, has to be acutely aware of the need to have a balanced approach in life. Personal filters can colour our view of reality and prevent us from reacting rationally in any given situation.

Accepting these few simple truths would save all of us a lot of needless heartache.

From the vantage point of where I am today, I know we cannot control the reactions of others. I also try to be more accepting of the failings of others. I realise if I want to hold on to my peace of mind, I have to let go of small-mindedness, irritation and anger. I may not always succeed. I have my weak moments. Who doesn't? But I never stop trying to maintain a more balanced outlook on life and on those around me.

I believe that in marriage, both partners' efforts and strengths should be recognised and valued. This mutual respect ensures a strong foundation between them. While Nick and I are no longer married, I hold respect for him. Like any married couple, we've had our share of highs and lows, but we value the friendship we've cultivated. We're now at a point where we understand each other better and are committed to nurturing our family and co-parenting as best we can.

THINGS TAKE TIME, AND TIME CAN CHANGE THINGS

Another life lesson that has proved to be a powerful guiding light for me is that we shouldn't be impatient when we want things to change. Things take time. Especially good things. A baby needs nine months to develop inside its mother's womb. Trees have to wait for the right season to produce fruits. And when they do produce them, the fruits need time to ripen. So also, a superstar athlete doesn't develop the capacity to break world records overnight. Some things just can't be rushed.

Healing takes time. Building a successful career takes time. Whether in our personal or business life, many things take time. It takes a while and sincere efforts to develop a more mature way of thinking, a more mature way of dealing with interpersonal relationships. So also, discovering your passion in life could take time, like in my case. I discovered mine after I became a successful businesswoman and was a mother of five.

If there is one virtue I've learned with time, it's patience. Numerous axioms endorse the virtue of patience. Rome was not built in a day. Slow and steady wins the race. What these seem to emphasise is that, if it's taking time to achieve a goal, don't lose heart. Don't ever let your passion to succeed wane. Don't give up.

Time changes things. They say you can't step into the same river twice. Just like a flowing river, time too, flows past, changing things and people in myriad ways. Some for the worse, some for the better. Ten years ago, I wasn't the same person. Ten years ago, I wasn't speaking on national TV in any country; I wasn't speaking at events across the world.

After years of feeling lost, resentful, scared, my thinking and my attitude toward people has changed. In the early years of my marriage to Nick, I used to feel his people and friends weren't accepting of me. Now, I try to understand everyone's reactions with a broader mind. I know that in life we are going to have experiences of all kinds and I shouldn't immediately react to them without pondering over things from all angles.

Today, I also know the value of having the courage to recognise our weaknesses and admit the areas that need to be worked on. Having such an approach helps us to improve, to become better, more balanced people.

So, let's face it. Let's accept the fact that people change with time. A doting boyfriend could change into a husband who takes you for granted. A relative you resented could turn out to be someone you like. A parent who had loads of patience with you when you behaved badly as a child could be hurt by even small acts of rudeness when they are older.

When it comes to family relationships, I can say from experience, the more understanding we show toward one another, the closer we'll remain to one another. It doesn't matter if it takes time to develop a spirit of understanding. Ultimately, it will help build stronger emotional bonds with loved ones and others in your life.

IT'S OKAY TO ADMIT YOU'RE IMPERFECT

To succeed in my goal of motivating others, I may need to persist with my own therapy sessions. But that's okay. We're all human. We don't have to be perfect. And that's another crucial lesson I've learned from training to be a motivational speaker. It's okay to have shortcomings, to be afraid, to be vulnerable. Having the courage to admit you're imperfect is a strength.

Accept and love yourself, flaws and all. That's essential. Like I mentioned in the life lesson about inner peace, only when you truly accept yourself will you be able to accept others. Only if you can love yourself will you be able to love and help others. What's important is, learning from our mistakes and sincerely working on our deficiencies.

Thankfully, I've come a long way from the days of experiencing low self-worth all the time. Today, I know that just because I have imperfections, just because I feel afraid sometimes or just because I make mistakes once in a while, that doesn't mean I'm not a courageous person or I'm not capable of putting my heart into motivating or coaching others or I have no qualities worthy of admiration or I'm not worth loving.

My focus today is on being the best version of myself I can be, for my own sake and also for the sake of my family and the people I want to help in their own personal quest for achieving success.

CHOOSE TO CHANGE YOUR NARRATIVE

We often tend to forget that it's in our hands to control and change the narrative of our life. Life is continually shaped by the choices we make. But we need to accept what happened in the past, including our mistakes and mourn our suffering. This may take time. But with time comes healing.

Changing your narrative also involves changing your mindset. But this cannot happen at the snap of your fingers. You will only change when you're ready for that change. And if you're still in the anger or mourning phase of your life, that is okay. You just need to be patient and allow your body to go through those emotions.

You may not be able to travel back in time and change the wrong decisions you made or the bad things that happened to you. But it is in your power to change the way you look at the past and your present circumstances. The perspective from which you look at these will control how optimistic you are and also the decisions you take in the present. You have the power and the freedom to look at obstacles in your path as challenges and decide how to lead your life today. You have the power to choose to change the narrative of your life and make the right choices for tomorrow. How you think will determine how you act. And how you act will ultimately shape the quality of your life. So, choose wisely.

Let me close with a story my mother once told me.

There was a king who had two birds. They were sitting on the branch of a tree when he commanded them to fly into the sky. One bird flew away and the other continued to sit on the branch, refusing to move. So, the king broke the branch of the tree and then the bird soared into the sky.

Sometimes, branches have to be broken for you to fly high.

My mother broke the branch I was sitting on and taught me to become resilient. Leaving home, I never understood her. But today, I do.

I hope this book will help break the branch you're sitting on so you may soar high and reach your goals. I hope adhering to the helpful suggestions and messages within the pages of this book will help you stay the course as you make your way ahead in life.

Remember: It doesn't matter if you have to start small. But don't be afraid to aim high in everything you do. Small thinking can only result in small achievements. To go far in life, find your passion, for only your passion can shape your purpose.

As we delve into part three of this book, I'm excited to share insights and tools that act as the compass guiding your journey. Initially, I had contemplated ending each chapter with a lesson, akin to signposts along the path. However, I wanted to maintain the seamless flow of my story for you.

So, here are these valuable tools for your consideration. Think of them as the sunrise – whether you choose to embrace them each morning or before you retire at night, they offer fresh perspectives and endless opportunities. These lessons, like the dawn or the gentle hush of nightfall, can light your way and accompany you through the chapters you have read.

I hope that exploring my experiences and life lessons has been as fulfilling for you as a reader as it has been for me as a motivational writer. This is a humble attempt to make a constructive difference in the lives of others. It is also a part of the legacy I wish to leave for my readers, audiences and clients, as well as my own loving family. I extend my love and prayers to each and every one of you, my brothers and sisters, and wish you soul-satisfying success in your own journey toward reaching your goals and enjoying renewed happiness.

PART THREE

CONVICTION IN ACTION: TOOLS FOR CHANGE

INNER STRENGTH

In the depths of your being, a luminous spark resides, a celestial glow, guiding you to conquer obstacles that dare to shadow your glow.

It's sad but true. Many of us live like a person who has an oyster shell but goes through life without opening it and discovering the pearl inside. Like that person, many of us fail to discover we possess something of great value. Inner strength. Like a pearl in an oyster, inner strength lies hidden deep within us, waiting to be discovered. Those who fail to discover and unleash it, will invariably feel crushed by the smallest misfortunes in life.

The reggae superstar Bob Marley once said something remarkable about inner strength. He said we never know how strong we are until being strong is the only choice we have. He was right. This happens with a lot of people. It happened in my life too. As a young child, I let adversity get to me. But not for long. Once I decided that living on my own was the only way out for me, I found the strength to stand up to any hard knocks that came my way. By the age of 20, I had already been toughened by multiple adversities. I even survived a near-death experience. Yes, I was scared for my life at that time, but I didn't fall to pieces.

Inner strength could also see you through the harshest difficulties. But building it requires determination. If you tend to get nervous easily, practise staying calm. Set a few minutes aside for yourself each day. Train yourself, like an athlete, with regularity and commitment. Focus on deep breathing exercises that keep you still and centred. Whether clearing your mind through reflection in solitude or practising meditation to connect with your inner self, a consistent routine of daily exercises like this will help you strengthen your inner core, **tap into your inner strength and be better equipped to meet adversities head-on**.

Fortunately, inner strength is independent of the horrible things that might have happened to you. It isn't controlled by failures or disappointments.

Developing inner strength, however, begins with self-love. It is self-love that makes us feel positive about ourselves, helps us realise our full potential, motivates us to become better versions of ourselves and keeps us mentally strong. Inner strength, in turn, sets the foundation for facing adversities with courage.

Life cannot always be a bed of roses. It can, of course, be wonderful at times but there are many other times that bring unexpected challenges. And when such challenges hit us, being prepared to take them on and handle ourselves in a way that is focused, determined, resilient and motivated, can make a world of difference.

As I dealt with the immediate impact of the abduction, that chapter in my story was also leaving deeper scars that would lead to further struggles with my own self-worth. But, by sharing my story now, I am acknowledging that every event, both traumatic and ecstatic, every memory and every person I have encountered along the way, has become part of the journey I am still exploring.

I am not alone in living a life that has been filled with heartache and self-doubt. What gives me hope for myself and anyone who has taken steps along a similar journey, is the knowledge that I am also not alone in being able to reach a place of healing.

BUILD YOUR INNER STRENGTH

To work on building your inner strength, first you need to be able to access your own power to self-regulate. Self-regulation is the ability to take control of your emotions and to understand and manage your responses to the things that are happening to you. It is the ability to centre both your body and your mind and calm yourself down. To do this, there are three key steps to follow:

STEP 1:

LEARN THE ART OF TACTICAL BREATHING

The practice of tactical breathing will enable you to stay grounded and concentrate more effectively in tense situations. Think of the breathing process as being like shifting your brain into its appropriate gear, as you navigate the events and circumstances around you. The act of breathing slowly and steadily calms the heart, lowers blood pressure and enhances your ability to think clearly.

Learning to breathe calmly through tactical breathing, for better control of your emotional responses, can be achieved. Practise these actions daily or whenever you need to feel calmer, stay regulated, and be more focused.

» Count to four, while inhaling through your nose

- » For four counts, hold your breath
- » Exhale through your mouth for four counts
- » After exhaling, hold your breath again for four counts
- » Now repeat the process three times.

When you have completed three cycles of breathing, consider the following technique – step 2 – for building inner strength:

STEP 2:

POSITIVE VISUALISATION

Sit comfortably, ensuring your feet are firmly grounded to the floor and let's practise some tactical breathing. After four counts of tactical breathing, reflect on a challenging time in your life, reassured by the sensation of safety from keeping your feet firmly planted on the floor.

Now…

Visualise a moment in time when you felt tremendously upset. Perhaps someone said or did something to offend you. Think about the rage you felt during this time. As you recall that rage and you become aware of your body tensing and your heart rate increasing, do three cycles of tactical breathing once again.

As you practise three cycles of tactical breathing, feel yourself becoming calmer, realising now you are not in that situation. You are here and now. Safe from harm.

Then, think about how much effort it has taken you to be here and now. Example: I am stronger today than I was yesterday. I am braver today than I was yesterday. I am bolder today than I was yesterday. I am wiser today than I was yesterday.

Now is the time to focus on your strengths. You have achieved something positive. By visualising your strengths, you are rewiring your brain through neuroplasticity.

We have more than 86 billion neurons in our brain and, through affirmations, prayer and meditation that enhance your ability to focus on your accomplishments, you are rewiring and retraining your brain to think positively, which builds inner strength. In time, you will see the effects of positive psychology and the difference it will make on your mental health.

Recognising your accomplishments is the key to building inner strength. In order to find strength within, you must be able to see the strengths first.

STEP 3:

CULTIVATE PATIENCE

Building inner strength requires patience and lots of it. Taking advantage of every learning opportunity life throws at you will help you grow each day; growth doesn't happen overnight. A child is only ready to walk in his or her own "right" time. Just as we understand that, we need to apply greater levels of patience to the development of maturity and learning the lessons we need to go through in life.

ACCEPTANCE

God, help me forgive what I can't change and move forward without pain.

Years later, as a young adult, after asking myself the same question perhaps hundreds of times, I still hadn't found the answer. Until finally, I found a way of cleansing myself of the feelings of victimhood, anger, misery and shame.

What helped me break free was acceptance. Let me clarify here that acceptance does not mean endorsing what happened in the past. It means accepting the reality of the situation. Instead of giving in to negative emotions and fighting what had happened to me, I now began to accept that the past cannot be undone. That what had happened, happened. No amount of fighting against it would change things for the better. I realised that negative feelings were constraining me, chaining me to my past, preventing me from moving on with my life. But acceptance set me free to look differently at myself and the world around me and at what had happened to me, encouraging me to take the first steps towards turning my life around.

To those of you who feel like the struggle to cope with your own trauma is driving you to the edge, I can assure you, acceptance is the empowering force that could help you deal with it in a constructive way. If you want to be healed from a traumatic past, if you want to stop your past from controlling you, you have to wake up to the fact that **it all begins with acceptance**.

With the acceptance of the fact that your pain is real and it is a normal reaction to what's happened, you must also accept that what's happened was not in your control and cannot be changed by brooding over it.

The causes of trauma are many. It could be paralysis following a fatal accident, losing your family members in a natural disaster, losing a loved one unexpectedly, experiencing the impact of family violence, childhood sexual abuse, abandonment, or lost trust.

But, as a powerful healing tool, acceptance doesn't discriminate. It needs to be part of any meaningful, sustainable way forward, no matter what adversity, pain or loss you've felt. The first step to overcoming trauma of any kind is acceptance.

In the case of some trauma, such as sexual abuse, this will also include accepting what happened to you wasn't your fault; it was the fault of the abuser.

A sad fact is survivors of childhood sexual abuse often must struggle to come to terms with it all their lives. But whatever the cause of your trauma, if you're finding it difficult to get over it, then it's time you talked to someone you can trust and who you believe cares for you. It could be a relative or a friend. It's important to accept, however, sometimes, your confidante may not have the ability or knowledge to help you heal.

My own mother, for instance, couldn't offer me the emotional support I badly needed. She reacted to traumatic events around her in the only way she knew how. If that is your experience and if you feel there's nobody you can trust with the secret you're carrying inside, then talk to a therapist.

Types of trauma do not discriminate either, sadly. Children

of both sexes are known to be targets of sexual abusers. Male survivors, however, are known to be more reluctant to seek help.

If you're one of them, remember that just because you were once sexually abused, doesn't make you less of a man. And neither does seeking professional help to deal with your trauma and move on.

Too often, we judge people for what are perceived as their 'failings'. People show what others see as weakness, or indecision, laziness, or an inability to 'cope' and are branded with sweeping assessments of their character and habits, without anyone wondering what might have led to their choices and responses.

But who are any of us to judge?

Acceptance can be a fine line that challenges us to understand that bad things do sometimes happen to good people and feelings of persecution and victimhood are not the best response.

Acceptance isn't about taking whatever people dish up to you unfairly without complaint or positive action. I think of it as a state of grace. When we can explore it, reflect on it and think about ways of inviting acceptance into our own lives which might help us heal, we open a door to fresh opportunities that could be life-changing and for the better.

Sometimes, acceptance also includes being able to accept people where they are at in life. I believe we are all in this life to grow and learn and we all learn different lessons at different times of our lives. An 80-year-old, for example, may be so stuck in old habits and behaviour patterns that they don't learn new, more positive things but, as frustrating as that realisation might feel, that's okay.

When we meet that person at that place and time and reality in their life, we don't have to accept their truth, but we can accept we are all at different stages in life.

OPEN YOUR MIND TO ACCEPTANCE

Embrace acceptance by acknowledging the aspects of life that are beyond your ability to change or control. It's important to recognise you can't dictate how others think; you can only share your perspectives. Picture this scenario: you're wearing sunglasses with a slight fog; removing them and wiping away the fog provides a clearer vision.

Consider this analogy in your interactions with others. Just like you can't remove the glasses from everyone around you, to make them see things exactly as you do, it's impossible to control their perspectives. Acceptance involves understanding that not everyone perceives the world through your lens. Finding peace begins with embracing this realisation and allowing others to see things in their unique way.

1. CHALLENGE NEGATIVE THOUGHTS

We all grapple with the monkey mind, that constant chatter of negative self-talk in our heads. The trick is to gain control over those thoughts and leveraging the benefits of neuroplasticity. Here's a three-step method:

1. Identify negative thoughts – Recognise when negative thoughts arise, such as saying, 'I am not good at my job.' Research shows that on average, humans have thousands of thoughts per day and acknowledging the negative ones is the first step. Neuroplasticity studies reveal our brain's capacity to rewire itself, allowing for the creation of new, positive neural pathways.
2. Challenge the thoughts – Question the truth of these thoughts. Research in cognitive psychology highlights that challenging negative thoughts can reshape our thinking patterns, promoting a more positive mindset. Neuroplasticity comes into play here, as the brain adapts and forms new connections based on the thoughts we reinforce.
3. Seek evidence and perspective – Prove to yourself whether these thoughts hold merit. Studies on cognitive restructuring emphasise gathering evidence to counteract negative beliefs. Understand that improvement areas exist for everyone, backed by the concept of the growth mindset. Neuroplasticity reinforces the idea that practising positive thinking can lead to lasting changes in brain structure.

Remember, questioning negative self-talk is not only a psychological tool but is supported by scientific findings and the neuroplasticity concept, offering a powerful step towards changing the way we think.

LEARN TO FORGIVE

Holding on to grudges and resentments can make it more difficult to accept things. As soon as you have forgiven yourself for the things you cannot change, you will find that forgiving others will aid you in releasing negative emotions and allowing your mind to be open to acceptance.

It is impossible to control anyone else's behaviours or to force them to change. As long as we are curious about ourselves, we can always choose to shift our attention inward. Every person views life differently, due to their unique experiences and lives lived. Cultivating forgiveness takes time and we must focus our attention inward on ourselves in order to be able to forgive. It is not our intention to condone or assume responsibility for the behaviour that causes our suffering. There is nothing we can do to change others or fix them, besides cultivating forgiveness for their shortcomings and understanding that we, as humans, are created imperfectly perfect.

SELF-FORGIVENESS

When I acted up by stealing, being dishonest, cutting class and trying to end my life, I was a troubled teenager exasperated by a sense of powerlessness that came from feeling I was not in control of what was happening in my life.

As I moved into adulthood, I cringed in disgust whenever I looked back at my teenage self.

How could I have hurt my parents when, really, I loved them? It took me a while to comprehend why I did what I did when I was younger. I realised my misbehaviour stemmed from hidden feelings of pain and loneliness.

By recognising that my behaviour was a direct response, I was able to replace indignation with empathy and repugnance with compassion. When I forgave my immature self and embraced my humanness, it was as if a weight had been lifted from my chest and I could breathe freely at last.

My body felt more relaxed and even my mind felt free from the tension that had caused me so much stress for so long. I could think more clearly and see things more positively. It was a powerful moment that taught me something profound.

I learnt that **with self-forgiveness comes healing**. By granting myself forgiveness, I changed the way I saw myself and the decisions I'd made. I wasn't bad, or stupid, or wrong. I was reacting to the hand I'd been dealt. I can't recommend self-forgiveness enough. Not only is it good for mental health, but it also boosts productivity and brings about a positive shift in the way we look at our past mistakes.

And the truth is, of course, that we ALL make mistakes, no matter what our age or circumstances. Mistakes, failures, wrong decisions, wrong choices, they're a part of life. What's important is to feel remorse for our wrongdoings, but in a constructive kind of way. Healthy remorse leads to positive change because, with it, comes a genuine willingness to **learn** from our mistakes.

As you go through life, you will, one day, find yourself at a crossroad or facing an unexpected hurdle. Making a rash decision may lead to doing something you'll regret. But when that does happen, don't allow yourself to be bogged down by unhealthy remorse that is more about beating yourself up over a bad choice, rather than acknowledging why you made the decision you did. That kind of remorse will get you nowhere.

Instead, use those experiences as stepping stones towards deeper learning and growth. As the legendary business magnate Henry Ford put it, the only real mistake is the one from which we learn nothing.

Self-forgiveness can be a challenging process, but it is an important step in healing and moving forward. Here are some steps that can help you to practise self-forgiveness:

1. Acknowledge your mistake

Recognise and accept you have made a mistake and take responsibility for it.

2. Understand the reasons behind your actions

Try to understand the underlying reasons for your behaviour. This can help you to see the situation in a different light and make it easier to forgive yourself.

3. Express remorse and restore yourself

Acknowledge the harm you may have caused and express remorse for your actions. Restore yourself with healing by making amends, even to yourself, which can change the narrative of the future. Learning from experience and growing as a person are essential to renewing oneself.

SELF-DETERMINATION

To some, it might seem that running away at 16 was an audacious decision on my part. It wasn't. The stifling atmosphere and the persistent lack of trust and understanding from my parents pushed me into taking control of my life while still in high school. I had no other option.

In all honesty, during the early months away from home, surviving on my own was a struggle. But the joy of being free to live my life the way I wanted to, make my own choices, decide where to live, what to wear, what to do in my spare time, was so immense, it made all the hardships seem worth it. What I was suddenly enjoying, perhaps a little too soon, was the opportunity to practise self-determination. Being self-determined let me discover what I could do on my own and later helped me make it as a successful entrepreneur.

As psychologists tell us, the ability to manage their own life is crucial for everyone and self-determination is a skill that should be learnt young and further developed in later years. What's more, people have a basic human need to be in control of their lives. Which is why self-determination is important for psychological health and for enjoying an overall better quality of life.

Self-determined people are known to be better at decision-making, problem-solving and goal setting. They are also more self-motivated than those who haven't had the opportunity to develop this skill.

The earlier we become self-determined, the better. So, if

you've got into the habit of constantly seeking validation for your decisions, do yourself a favour and try and get out of it as soon as you can. In my case, I was constantly seeking validation, but failing to receive it from those nearest to me – my own parents. To help myself believe I truly was good enough and not worthless, I began needing it from others.

The good news is, once you start making decisions for yourself, you'll soon realise that **self-determination sets you free**. Free to take action without depending on the opinions of others, free to realise your self-worth and free to discover your strengths and weaknesses all by yourself.

However, if you're still struggling to cope with extreme trauma, it would be hard to become self-determined without professional help. Working with a trained psychologist could help you dig deep, right to the root of your problems and fears. Once you've done that, you will have a greater understanding of what made you the way you are. With the right therapy, you'll be able to work through your doubts and realise the power to overcome trauma truly lies within you.

Self-determination also requires courage.

It takes courage to put your needs first, whatever they may be and it takes courage to live your life the way you want to. When it comes to putting bold decisions into positive action, especially with respect to your future, you'll need to have the courage to take risks. But before things in your life can get to that stage, you'll need to become accustomed to making smaller decisions independently.

Yes, you might make mistakes along the way, but just like taking a few stumbles is a part of how a toddler learns to walk, you'll learn from those mistakes and only grow stronger.

LIVING WITH SELF-DETERMINATION

Living with self-determination means taking control of your life and making choices that align with your values, goals and aspirations.

Here are some steps that can help you live with genuine self-determination:

1. Define your values and goals

Take the time to understand what is important to you and what you want to achieve. This can help you make choices that align with your values and goals.

2. Take ownership of your choices and gain mastery

Take responsibility for the choices you make and the actions you take. This can help you feel in control of your life and more self-determined. Self-determination can be built by gaining mastery. Become skilled in areas that matter to you. Learn as much as possible about the subject and improve your skills, whether you have a strong interest in it or not.

3. Take risks

Taking risks can help you grow and learn. Don't be afraid to step out of your comfort zone and try new things. The less fear you have, the more fearless you will be.

MAGICAL THINKING

May self-awareness shine brighter than infatuation's illusions. In clarity, find the truth of genuine love.

In my early adult life, I found comfort in illusions, relying on friendships to stave off the fear of loneliness. This coping mechanism became especially crucial when I left home, driven by a deep-seated terror of being alone.

The yearning for family led me to construct an imaginary, tight-knit kinship in my mind, blurring the boundaries between friends and family.

It wasn't until my late 40s that I realised my mind harboured thoughts of limerence and infatuation—forms of magical thinking born from trauma.

Trauma can impact the brain in various ways, including magical thinking. For instance, feeling in love with someone, even if they aren't suitable for you. Fantasising about their greatness and giving them importance, even if they don't reciprocate.

In my pursuit of love, I discovered that genuine love starts from within. This realisation took time, as did the process of forgiving myself for what I didn't understand.

I delve into the concept of 'Limerence', a coping mechanism born from trauma. It's like the brain turns to magical thinking to escape pain, creating a world of love and acceptance, even if it's not real. We assign titles to people, turning friends into family and aunts and uncles into surrogate parents. However, finding fulfilment within ourselves is the key.

'Magical Thinking' offers solace in times of trauma, creating dreamlike feelings of false affections. For instance, seeking comfort in sweet words during an unhappy marriage. It may seem like love, but it often stems from a yearning for affection rooted in childhood lacks.

We all have triggers, both bad and good. Sometimes, someone says something to upset us, triggering a surge of rage within. Recognising this, we take the time to calm down. However, what happens when someone utters words your subconscious craves to hear, like 'I love you, I need you and you are the moon in my sky'? These longed-for expressions, usually from parents, can spark 'magical thinking' or limerence.

Recognising our triggers allows us to see when we're thinking unrealistically and how it impacts our lives. To overcome limerence, it's essential to identify the signs that indicate we're not thinking clearly.

How to stop limerence and move into reality:

The stories we tell ourselves can be so powerful and the psychological effect from trauma, known as 'limerence' can leave lasting scars.

Symptoms of limerence include craving love, creating fantasies and intrusive thinking about love. Fear of rejection is also a component. Limerence often occurs when there are cracks in our primary relationship and is also a symptom of **relational trauma from early life attachment wounds.** Jumping ship to a new relationship is not the answer to limerence. A better response is to invest our energy in how we relate to our partner and how they relate to us.

Trauma can have a significant impact on a person's emotional and psychological well-being and it can affect the way they perceive and interact with others, including in romantic relationships.

However, it is not clear if trauma directly leads to limerence, which is a state of intense romantic attraction or infatuation.

What is known is that trauma can disrupt a person's emotional regulation and make them more susceptible to intense and unstable emotions. This can cause them to become fixated on a person as a source of comfort and security, and therefore experience intense feelings of limerence.

Additionally, trauma can also affect a person's ability to form healthy relationships and they may be more likely to engage in unhealthy or unreciprocated relationships, which may increase the chances of developing limerence.

However, it's also important to note that people can experience limerence in a variety of situations and not just as a result of trauma. Limerence can happen to anyone, regardless of their past experiences.

If you are experiencing limerence and trauma, seeking professional help to address both issues is strongly recommended. A therapist or counsellor can help you understand and work through your feelings and also help you develop healthier coping mechanisms and relationship patterns.

It can be difficult to stop limerence but there are steps you can take to move into reality:

1. Recognise the feelings

Strive for equilibrium in your relationships, avoiding overcommitment or excessiveness. Aim to reciprocate the level of effort and engagement you receive from others. For instance, if someone isn't initiating calls, resist the urge to constantly reach out. Maintain a balanced dynamic in relationships to prevent potential resentment. Assess the role of the person you hold limerence for, ensuring feelings and actions are mutually reciprocated. Beware of making excuses, as it might indicate the influence of limerence.

Acknowledge that you are experiencing limerence and understand that it is a natural, but temporary, state of mind.

2. Challenge your thoughts and give yourself time

Limerence can cause you to idealise the person you are attracted to. Challenge this idealisation by focusing on the person's flaws and reality. It's important to give yourself time because limerence can be intense, but it is a temporary state of mind. Give yourself time and be patient with the process of moving on.

3. Be honest with yourself

Be honest with yourself about your feelings and the likelihood of the relationship working. It's important to not let limerence cloud your judgement. Remember, it's important to understand that limerence is not the same as love and it is not sustainable in the long run. The feelings will subside with time and it's important to focus on your own growth and well-being as you move into reality.

RESOURCEFULNESS

Resourcefulness is an important life skill and one that I developed at a very young age. Whether it was the creative way I made a little money go a long way while trying to turn my rental flats into homes, even on a shoestring budget, or leveraging my love of cooking to plan and launch a catering business and become more financially independent, I proved I had the ability to optimise all available resources to solve problems and get the desired results.

SURVIVORS MASTER THE ART OF RESOURCEFULNESS

When confronted with an obstacle, survivors can tap into out-of-the-box thinking and come up with an innovative way of transcending it. Conversely, those who don't have a 'resourceful mindset' are more likely to be frustrated by a roadblock and, consequently, give up on their dreams.

But resourcefulness isn't one of those traits that **only** business leaders should have; it's a valuable life skill as well. Luckily, it's not an inherited trait. I firmly believe that it's one that any person can learn. A mindset anyone can acquire. You just have to shift your thinking in times of trouble.

When they want something bad enough, most people

spontaneously start looking for alternative ways to get it. They won't stop till they've found what they're looking for. That's because resourcefulness makes you focus on finding a solution, not on worrying about the problem.

Resourceful people are known to respond better to adversity – therefore proving the truth in the saying about adversity being the best teacher and that it has the potential to bring out the best in you.

In my own life, when push came to shove, it was resourcefulness that helped me find ways to augment the modest support I received from Centrelink. Resourcefulness kept me going and kept my never-say-die attitude alive and kicking as a child. This habit gave me the confidence to think of even more daring solutions to keep my head above water in the years to come.

REWARD YOURSELF FOR RESOURCEFULNESS

Rewarding yourself for being resourceful can be a great way to recognise your efforts and motivate you to continue using your resourcefulness in the future.

1. Identify your resourceful actions

Take note of the actions you have taken that demonstrate resourcefulness. This can include things like finding a solution to a difficult problem, being resourceful with limited resources, or being creative in your approach to a task.

2. Set rewards

Decide on rewards that align with your values and goals. These can include tangible rewards like treating yourself to a new book or an experience reward, such as a day trip or a night out somewhere special.

3. Build your knowledge through education

There is no doubt that education plays a critical role in enabling us to be resourceful, as knowledge and skills are required. You will become an informed decision-maker, a critical thinker and a problem-solver through education.

Taking the time to recognise and value your resourcefulness is a crucial step. The more resourceful you become, the better version of yourself you will be.

PRACTICAL THINKING

Fortunately for me, I adopted a practical approach to facing the harsh realities of my new life away from home right from the time I suddenly had to fend for myself at 16. Having accepted I had no other option, I decided to be practical about it. Whether it was selecting accommodation, buying furniture, handling multiple jobs to support myself financially, I had to make all these decisions level-headedly.

When I agreed to get married, it was so that my child could grow up in what I saw as a 'proper' family – with two parents. I also hoped that becoming a father would have a positive influence on Gaz. I was realistic enough to know Gaz wouldn't change his abusive ways. But I was willing to take that risk because the traditional thinking that was so deeply ingrained in me – that a child should be raised with both its mother and father – clouded my judgement.

When I think back to that time now, I realise that, in difficult situations, we tend to think of what the best decision could be, under the given circumstances. Our perceptions of what those 'best' decisions might be are controlled by the mindset we hold at that time.

Today, we cannot change what happened in the past, but instead of admonishing ourselves for past mistakes, we have the power to change the way we think of ourselves. Being kind to ourselves for past choices is, in a way, thinking practically in the present.

Practical-minded people see the world as it is, with all its imperfections and uncertainties. But they're not pessimists. While pessimism is bad for mental health, being practical means openly acknowledging the truth.

Practical thinking keeps you grounded, keeps you balanced, keeps you from having unrealistic expectations and setting yourself up for disappointment. Practical thinkers don't make decisions based on emotions, but on logic and facts. They're prepared for any eventuality, often having a back-up plan ready.

A practical approach has special significance for anyone craving entrepreneurial success, because business-minded people inevitably launch their ventures by taking several risks. The smart ones take informed risks. But in general, for new businesses, risk **is** the name of the game. Entrepreneurs, therefore, must think practically from the word 'go' and be prepared to adapt to failures.

As a practical person, you might dream big, but always set realistic goals for yourself. You acknowledge that there may be hardships and roadblocks along the way. And, on encountering these, you take a practical approach towards overcoming them. That is, you will most likely reassess your earlier strategy and make the necessary changes for the road ahead, at the same time learning from the problems you faced. That's what being practical is all about.

A practical person tries to come up with plans that will work in the real world. She might not get everything right all the time, but when her plans hit an unforeseen obstacle or she sees they're not producing the desired results, she'll be willing to course-correct. A few years later, instead of continuing along a path that could only lead to ruin, I course-corrected too. And that was what made all the difference.

MAKE PRACTICAL THINKING A DAILY HABIT

Making practical thinking a daily habit can help you approach problems and decisions with a clear and logical mindset.

1. Start small

Begin by applying practical thinking to small, manageable tasks. As you become more comfortable with the process, you can gradually apply it to more complex problems and decisions.

2. Breakdown and reflect

Break down complex problems into smaller, more manageable parts. This can make it easier to approach the problem with a practical mindset. Reflect on the decisions you make and consider the practicality of the outcome. This can help you identify areas for improvement and make better decisions in the future.

3. Feedback matters

Seek feedback from others on your practical thinking skills. This can help you identify areas for improvement and learn from others.

It takes practice and persistence to develop the habit of practical thinking and the ability to approach problems and decisions logically and clearly.

RESILIENCE

Don't judge me by my accomplishments, but by the kindness of my heart.

In life, it is resilience that gives us the fortitude to confront adversities unhesitatingly and take them on the chin. Agreed, we need inner strength to overcome adversities too, but it is resilience that helps us bounce back after being dealt knockout blows. While it isn't enough to just be mentally strong, we must remember that, without mental toughness we cannot develop resilience.

Resilient people have an unwavering belief in their abilities. They aren't afraid of challenges and nor do they run away from them. When they have a setback, rather than mourning over their failure, they reflect on where they've gone wrong and have the courage to take a fresh stab at overcoming the obstacles in their path, even daring to try a new approach to tackle an old adversity.

We need to develop qualities like that to be resilient: the honesty and forthrightness to acknowledge our mistakes, the courage to get up and fight again and a streak of daring that pushes us to attempt new things and find new roads to move ahead.

Resilience is key to thriving in challenging times.

It helps us stay calm under pressure. Stress, on the other hand, keeps us from becoming resilient. It impairs the brain's ability to think clearly when faced with difficulties. With that reality to guide you, one of the first steps towards developing resilience is to keep your stress levels down. You could do this by regularly setting time aside for doing things that help you relax and calm down. It doesn't have to be spectacular or costly. Simply going for a stroll or listening to music you enjoy could be the calming activity you need. Daily exercise, getting a good night's sleep and eating a nutritious diet are other small things that can make a big difference – especially when we make them a habitual part of our ongoing commitment to better health and the stress-relieving benefits it delivers.

I went through terrifying times in my relationship with Gaz: first as his girlfriend, when he assaulted me so badly that he changed my face forever; then as his wife, when he beat me mercilessly for the most trivial reasons.

As cliched and simplistic as it might seem, a critical part of my survival hinged on repeatedly reminding myself that, although he could break my bones, he could never break my spirit.

In those difficult early days of marriage, I plodded on, pretending to be a willing part of that toxic partnership, even though I knew I would have to take a bold decision regarding our union someday. And when that day eventually came, it was for the wellbeing and safety of both my son and myself.

I proved I had the mettle and courage to stand up to an abusive husband and walk out of my sham marriage with my head held high, my resilient mindset intact, and dreams – big dreams! – of becoming an achiever, entrenched firmly in my mind and heart. In fact, I surprised myself when I successfully planned and staged a world-class event, completely under my own steam.

That's what bouncing back looked like for me. Of course, for other people, it may come in simpler, more everyday forms or, perhaps, something even bigger.

Whatever bouncing back might mean to you, if you treat resilience like a muscle that needs strengthening and conditioning, it will eventually feel strong enough to help you take positive action.

Building resilience during challenging times is a process that involves developing strategies to cope with stress and adversity.

1. Sleep enough

Getting the right amount of sleep is necessary for emotional regulation, anxiety reduction and mood improvement. Adults should have between 7-9 hours of quality sleep and children and teenagers should get between 8-10 hours. A good night's sleep will help you become more resilient.

2. Exercise builds resilience

Exercise releases endorphins, which are brain chemicals that improve mood and reduce anxiety and depression.

3. Avoid distractions

As with everything in life, we need balance so we can take the time to cultivate what we need to do for ourselves to build self-resilience. Being there for all your friends' problems without boundaries and limits can be exhausting and it prevents you from taking care of yourself.

If you have time, perhaps you could read more books or watch a movie by yourself.

Developing resilience requires time for you to reflect on ways you can grow to become more at peace.

With practice and patience, you can learn to cope with stress and adversity and build the resilience you need to thrive in challenging times.

RESPONSIBILITY

'Richness is not having belongings, but richness is the contentment of the soul'
– Prophet Muhammad (Peace Be Upon Him)

Substance abuse was playing havoc with my mind and causing more turmoil in my already troubled life. The anxiety I felt in those brief spells of separation from Adam were making me sink deeper into drug addiction as a form of self-medication. Despite that, I did not want to surrender the responsibility of looking after and protecting him. Instead, I fought for him and tried to be the only one responsible for taking care of him. My suicide attempt was done in a moment of absolute weakness, driven by my self-pitying belief that my son would be better off without a mother like me.

Instead of caring properly for myself, I put myself through even greater stress by working multiple jobs so I could earn enough to better support my son and myself all on my own. Unfortunately, the drugs I took got in the way of being the best mother I could be, even though, at the time, my clouded judgement meant I justified my actions and still believed I was offering him great maternal care.

Acting responsibly may not always be easy. But responsible people do what's the right thing to be done without hesitation and without counting the cost. **Taking responsibility shows**

a determination to take charge. While those who shirk their responsibilities are seen as untrustworthy and incapable of following through on their commitments, responsible behaviour is commonly linked to positive qualities like reliability and uprightness. When you take up your responsibilities gladly, you not only begin to respect yourself more, you earn the respect of others as well.

Whether you're a parent, spouse, friend, employee or business leader, taking your responsibilities seriously will give you the strength to create sustainable, positive changes into your life and help you mature as an individual.

Becoming more responsible in your life involves making choices that consider the impact on yourself, others and the environment.

1. Honesty and responsibility

Be honest and keep your promises to yourself and others. This can help you build trust and be more reliable. Take responsibility for your actions and their consequences. This can help you learn from mistakes and make more responsible choices in the future.

2. Help others

Help others in your community or in need. This can help you become more empathetic and responsible towards others.

3. Be environmentally conscious

Be environmentally conscious by reducing your carbon footprint, recycling and using sustainable products. This can help you nurture a broader view of your place in the world and the responsibility you have to yourself and others.

4. Avoid being easily swayed by others

Make your own decisions and don't be easily swayed by what you think will make you the coolest person in the room. Make your own decisions, based on your understanding of right and wrong.

5. Say 'no' to drugs and alcohol

Drugs and alcohol can lead to severe depression. The reason for this is that, for people who have had severe trauma in their life, their tendency to be stuck in flight, fight, freeze or fawn mode can be incredibly taxing on their nervous system.

With every drink (or perception-altering drug), the nervous system is relaxed and the feeling is freeing on the body so controlling the drinks or substance becomes difficult. One too many drinks, or abuse of drugs, can then trigger side effects such as depression and tiredness. The effects of alcohol and substance abuse on suicidal behaviour are many. Suicide is more likely to occur in people who are dependent on substances. Their depression is accompanied by social and financial problems. People who participate in high-risk behaviours, such as self-harm, are prone to substance abuse and addiction. Living an alcohol-free and drug-free life can help you live a more proactive life and you will begin to think with much more clarity.

Remember, becoming more responsible takes time and effort, but with practice and patience, you can make choices that are good for yourself, others and the environment.

A WINNING MINDSET

If you aim for the treetops, you may hit the ground, but if you aim for the stars, you will reach the treetops.

All of us will find ourselves battling challenges at some time or another. Life isn't always going to be smooth sailing. However, while some people feel crushed by adversities, others find a way to overcome them. The root cause of this difference in behaviour is their mindset. It is your mindset that controls the way you look at challenges. Inevitably, those who emerge successful, out of even the worst-case scenarios, are those who have a winning mindset. Determined not to give up on their dreams, they strive tirelessly and do what it takes to find a solution to their problem.

While others are full of doubts, those with a winning mindset believe no obstacle is insurmountable and if they failed to go past it before, they just might have to deal with it differently, more intelligently, to succeed.

If I was asked to contribute my very own quote related to the power of a winning mindset, it would be this one:

The power of mind shift can take you places you never thought imaginable.

When I took on the task of managing a café that was struggling to stay afloat, what helped me rise to the challenge was the winning mindset I'd been unconsciously cultivating. Whether it was the small catering business I started as a strategy for survival, the success I'd achieved with the international beauty pageant or the transformation of Piccolo Café, my focus was always on winning. I saw to it that my mind was always buzzing with positive thoughts. On taking over the running of my brother's café, I acknowledged I had a lot to learn about the business and was willing to put in the hard work to accomplish that. At the same time, I thought of how I could leverage my strengths to make things that much easier for me.

It isn't difficult to retrain your mind to think like a winner. The first thing you need to make this happen, is the hunger to succeed. Secondly, you need to believe in your ability to win. According to psychologists, we become what we think we are. If you think you can never win, you'll continue to be an underachiever. If you think you can only be an average Jane or Joe, that's what you'll stay for the rest of your life. Instead, if you have a positive image of yourself, it will be easier for you to grow in confidence and self-belief. The third thing that's needed is getting into the habit of thinking positively, whatever the circumstances.

A winning mindset keeps you optimistic. It motivates you to acquire new skills and keeps you from giving up when times are difficult. More importantly, you need to **develop a winning mindset to discover your full potential**. Knowing what you're truly capable of will, in turn, change the way you respond to failure and challenging situations. Ultimately, tapping into your full potential will motivate you to put in the hard work to overcome adversities and achieve your goals.

Nurturing a high-performance mindset involves developing the attitudes, beliefs and behaviours that can help you achieve your goals and succeed in your endeavours. Here are three practical steps to help you nurture a winning mindset:

1. Set clear goals and develop a growth mindset

Set clear, specific and achievable goals for yourself. This will give you something to work towards and provide a greater sense of direction. Adopt a mindset that focuses on learning and growth, rather than perfection and fixed abilities. This will help you become more adaptable and resilient in the face of challenges.

2. Clear your space and your mind

Make your bed and clean your space daily. A clutter-free environment will allow you to think

more clearly. The habit of making your bed sets the tone for the day, because when you feel good about your environment, you release happy endorphins that put you in a positive mood.

3. Practice visualisation through prayer and or meditation

Practice visualisation and imagine yourself achieving your goals. This can help you stay focused and more motivated. Prayer can help to create a sense of calm and inner peace, which can be beneficial when nurturing a high-performance mindset.

THE COURAGE OF CONVICTION

Conviction gives you the courage to act bravely, to be committed to doing what you think is right, disregarding criticism, peer pressure, or the risk of being victimised. It also gives you the power to overcome the resistance, to doing something you absolutely should do.

It was conviction that ultimately helped me kick my drug habit. Conviction also helped me realise that a good man had entered my life and enabled me to accept that what we felt for each other was wholesome and genuine. It led me into confidently starting a new life with Nick.

The courage of conviction points you in the right direction.

Without conviction, your attempts to achieve success would be directionless, jaded and half-hearted. Any initiative you take without conviction will fail to produce the desired results. Even easily attainable goals will seem out of your reach. And, in time, the obstacles in your path could become bigger and seem like permanent barriers between you and success.

When faced with a dilemma in life, when it's unclear which road would be a better choice, it is unwise to make an impulsive decision too hastily. Instead, take the time to consider where each road could lead you. Seeking assurance of what the consequences of following each path might be can help you make a clearer, more informed decision. Such a decision can only be reached through conviction.

So, how can you be truly convinced about something

being right for you? Conviction can only come from the full knowledge of an idea or action and having a clear understanding of its purpose. Successful people, whether they're homemakers, professionals or business leaders, produce commendable results because their every action is driven by conviction. They're not only convinced about what action they should take; they have the courage to act on their convictions. Like the philosopher, Thomas Carlyle, said, 'Conviction is worthless unless it is converted into conduct.'

Conviction in life is important because it helps us overcome indecisiveness. It ensures we don't get easily swayed by others into doing something that may not be in our best interests. It also fires us with the zeal to give our all to whatever tasks we undertake.

Taking moments to pause and reflect on the quality of your life is always a positive habit. Are you just drifting from day to day, leading a bland existence? Or is yours a life of purpose, guided by robust personal convictions?

Living with conviction means having strong beliefs and being willing to stand by them, even in the face of opposition or uncertainty. One way to live with conviction is to regularly examine and reflect on your values and beliefs and to make sure they align with your actions and decisions. It also means being willing to act in support of your beliefs and being open to learning and growth.

Additionally, staying true to yourself and standing up for what you believe in, while being respectful of other people's perspectives and beliefs, is important in living a life with conviction.

1. Identify your values and beliefs
Take some time to reflect on what is most important to you

in life. What are your core values and beliefs? Write them down and make sure they align with your actions and decisions. You should be true to yourself, stand up for what you believe in and respect other people's perspectives and beliefs.

2. Be willing to take action

Living with conviction means being willing to take action in support of your beliefs. This could be as simple as speaking up when you hear something you disagree with, or as complex as committing to a long-term project that aligns with your values.

3. Stay informed and educated

Keep yourself informed about the issues that align with your beliefs and be willing to learn more about them. The more you know, the more effectively you can advocate for your beliefs. Living with conviction means being willing to face challenges and criticism. It can be difficult to stand up for what you believe in but remember that you are doing so because you believe it is the right thing to do.

FOCUS

*Focus breeds dedication and dedication
breeds accomplishment.*

Imagine someone driving a car and admiring the scenery or constantly speaking into her mobile phone instead of focusing on what she's doing at that moment ie., driving. She's obviously putting herself at risk of getting into an accident and suffering serious injuries or even losing her life. The truth is, you can pay a high price for losing focus in life.

Focus is a critical thinking skill. Focusing on what you've chosen to do will help you do it better and get more done in less time. Being able to achieve greater focus will enhance your problem-solving skills and productivity, help you stay in the moment and enable you to attain your goals faster. Losing focus, on the other hand, can result in losing sight of your goals and becoming frustrated.

Interestingly, the ability to focus is also one of the techniques practised for coping with stress and an overactive fight-or-flight response. Those who've experienced trauma tend to repeatedly go into fight-or-flight mode because they feel threatened more often, even in non-threatening circumstances. Focusing on calming words or serene images are key components of focus-related techniques, like meditation and breathing exercises, which are also a small thing that can have a big impact.

Sports superstars are excellent examples of the heights a single-minded focus on a goal can take someone to. What helps them stick to their rigorous training regimens is focus.

Staying focused could call for sacrifices, greater self-control and stronger willpower. It isn't easy. But like any other skill, you can get better at it through practice.

Choosing to stay focused also involves getting your priorities right. To achieve your goals, you need to zero in on what's most important to you.

When Nick and I started a new life together, our focus was on making a success of our marriage, despite the two of us having different religious and cultural backgrounds. Like all marriages, ours had ups and downs too, but our focus on keeping our marriage on track kept us going. For the same reason, I tried to build a healthy relationship with my mother-in-law, even though she was cold toward me in the early years of my relationship with Nick. I could have chosen to focus on trivial things that annoyed me. To my credit, I didn't.

Focus matters. Choose yours wisely

If leading a contented life is what you want, focus on the positive things in your life and refrain from dwelling on negative thoughts. If it's important to you to mend fences with a loved one, focus on their good qualities, not their flaws. What you focus on could make the difference between failure and success, between misery and happiness.

PRACTICAL WAYS TO SHARPEN YOUR FOCUS

1. Passion sharpens focus

Being passionate about your work can increase your focus. A passion for your work can increase engagement and motivation, resulting in better concentration and focus. Passion for your work leads to increased commitment, which results in improved performance and productivity. Furthermore, staying motivated and overcoming obstacles can be easier when doing something you love.

2. Sharing too much can disrupt focus

When you share your projects with others, it can have both positive and negative effects on your focus. The benefits of talking about your projects include staying accountable, staying motivated and coming up with new ideas. Additionally, too many people talking about your projects can lead to interruptions and distractions, making it difficult to concentrate. You may also become demotivated and lose focus if you share your project too early, which may result in criticism and negative feedback.

Maintaining a balance between sharing and keeping your projects private is important. Take time to focus on your work without distractions by sharing your projects with a few trusted friends or colleagues who can provide helpful feedback.

Communication is also vital in setting boundaries and communicating your need for privacy and focus.

3. Be proactive and creative with your thoughts

Start a morning journal to outline your thoughts, goals, and tasks for the day, and check off each completed item to track your progress.

PERSEVERANCE

It's interesting how babies learn to walk. No one has to tell them what to do. Despite falling down numerous times, bruising themselves, getting hurt and often, even howling with pain, they remain unfazed by the failed attempts and keep getting up to try again.

Our brains are wired to keep trying till we succeed. Sadly, when we grow up, before we can grasp the basics, we're impatient to produce a masterpiece. We want to be able to boast of achieving something great without taking the trouble to learn or putting in the required hours of hard work and practice.

But success isn't an overnight thing. Yes, it needs inspiration, but it also needs the proverbial 99 percent perspiration. If we think we can find a shortcut to success, we're only fooling ourselves. Unfortunately, unlike little babies, many people are turned off by early failures. They start a task, high on enthusiasm, but when they find it isn't as easy as they'd thought it would be, they make excuses for their slow progress and give up trying.

History, however, is full of stories of great and outstanding achievements that followed keeping to the task in the face of obstacles and failures. These stories testify that **perseverance smooths the path to success**. Perseverance is a wonderful skill to have at all stages of life.

Thomas Edison's story is a remarkable example of perseverance. As a young boy, his teacher sent a note home to his mother claiming he was too stupid to learn anything. He was actually partially deaf. His mother's response? 'I'll teach him myself.' Edison's remarkable perseverance and numerous inventions make his story truly inspiring.

So, Edison's story actually begins with the perseverance of his mother. He invented the first practical light bulb after years of research and thousands of failed attempts! When a reporter asked about the numerous disappointments, he refused to accept them as failures, saying he'd found ten thousand ways that wouldn't work.

When I pursued the legal process of bringing Gaz to court to face justice, it was no easy task. What I did was not as outstanding as Edison's achievement. But though it took almost two years and loads of legwork, patiently tracing old medical records and finding the doctors who'd treated me a decade earlier, I persisted with collecting all kinds of data, despite getting pregnant along the way, and testified in court in an advanced state of pregnancy, sticking with it till justice was delivered. And that's exactly what perseverance is. To stay the course till the goal is reached.

Here are a few ways to develop a routine of perseverance:

1. Your history is fuel

a) Think about both the positive and negative experiences you have had in the past. Make use of those lessons and insights to inform your future and goals. By reflecting on the negative parts of your life, you can use them as fuel for a better future by developing perseverance as a motivation to achieve those goals.

Once you understand your motivations…

b) Remember to try to set small, achievable goals and gradually increase the difficulty as you gain confidence and momentum towards consistent perseverance.

2. Habit and perseverance

The key to developing any habit is consistency, which leads to perseverance. When it comes to getting closer to achieving your goals, put perseverance into practice every day, even if it is just for a few minutes. Staying motivated and focused is easier when you develop a repetitive habit of taking strategic actions that bring you closer to your goal.

A brain region associated with movement and coordination is the basal ganglia, where habits are formed. By repeating behaviours, the basal ganglia create connections between different parts of the brain, allowing the behaviour to become automatic.

The process of habituation occurs in three stages:

- **The cue:** A specific situation or context that triggers the behaviour.
- **The routine:** The behaviour itself.
- **The reward:** The positive outcome that reinforces the behaviour.

With repetition, the connections between the cue, the routine and the reward become stronger, making the behaviour more automatic.

When you repeat a certain behaviour consistently over time, you develop repetitive habits. For a behaviour to become automatic, a person must repeat it continuously. The result is, it becomes easier to continue performing the behaviour, despite obstacles or distractions, which is core to perseverance.

3. Ask yourself why?

Why do you want to achieve a goal? Why will it make your life better? Why are you passionate about achieving your dreams?

When you understand why you have to do something and how it will impact your life for the better, only then will you develop and nurture the perseverance to make it happen. Asking yourself this important question leads to perseverance, which is one of the most powerful and effective tools to help you overcome the challenges of your past and work towards a better future.

SELF-ESTEEM

No one is worthless. All of us have value. All of us are worth something.

Do you think a surgeon's work makes him more important than a school teacher? They both play different, but important, roles in society. Having clarified that, let's look at the difference between self-worth and self-esteem. Although these two are interconnected and are often used interchangeably, there's a fine line between them. Self-worth refers to the knowledge of your worth – your value as a person. Self-esteem is related to how you think of yourself. So, how are they connected? Well, a sense of self-worth can help overcome low self-esteem.

Now let's focus on self-esteem and how it impacts our life. **Self-esteem boosts morale.** It also controls how you think of yourself and others, how you feel, how you interact with others, it affects your outlook on life itself. And don't ever forget that self-esteem can be a potent motivator as well.

Like true happiness, the feeling of self-esteem springs from within you. It doesn't come from the way others treat you or things that happen to you. So, even if someone hurts or humiliates you, you can still have high self-esteem. You can still find ways to piece yourself together a little at a time, seeking therapy, if necessary.

However, the reverse is also true. Often, even when everything in life is going well for people, as happened later on in my life, they may still have low self-esteem. It all depends on the way they think.

You don't need to have low self-esteem if you're not earning as much as someone else, or if you're not as rich, beautiful or smart as someone else. Low self-esteem will make you think poorly of yourself, make you think you're not worthy enough. A high self-esteem, on the other hand, inspires you to respect yourself, acknowledge your capabilities and achievements and become more optimistic.

So, for a start, we need to dispense with negative thoughts about ourselves. Like Rumi said:

Be like a tree and let the dead leaves drop.

Negative thoughts are like dead leaves. So just do the smart thing and drop them. Instead, flood your mind with positive thoughts. They will motivate you to believe in yourself and heighten your sense of self-esteem. I'm telling you this with full conviction. It was belief in myself and my capabilities and my sense of self-esteem that led me to think of new possibilities in my life.

Ways to recognise and celebrate your worth:

1. Love who you are, from the inside

In our childhood, we absorb what others say about us as true. If we are told we are unkind, worthless, or worse, then we will believe it. Self-worth is the foundation on which self-esteem is built. You are worth celebrating for what you are made of (inside) – your heart and soul.

Kindness, warmth and humility are more valuable than success and ego.

2. Your story matters

Don't forget the importance of your story. Your voice is

significant; speaking up and standing up for issues that matter to you is a meaningful way to honour your worth. Be sure to use your voice to speak up and stand up for what you believe in, regardless of what others around you may think. When you speak up for what matters to you, you are celebrating your worth in the most authentic way.

3. Assume equal power (so you are not above or below others)

Equal rights for all people are certainly a way of demonstrating your own self-worth, as it shows you value and respect all individuals. Our belief in the equality and rights of others can be an extension of our self-worth, as we acknowledge and respect their humanity. Aside from standing up for what is just and right, advocating for and working towards, the equality of marginalised and oppressed communities can also contribute to a sense of personal self-worth.

COMMITMENT

Commit to self-improvement, for in forgiving yourself and others, we find the path to a better version of who we are.

The journey of supporting and nourishing relationships, and of life itself, is never smooth all the way or all the time. We know that. The going can get tough, even precarious. But we have to keep going, taking ups and downs in our stride. The sustaining force that can help us persist through the journey is commitment.

When you feel like throwing in the towel, when you feel you don't have the energy to continue, commitment will keep you moving forward. When a bridge gets broken, commitment helps fix it. When you hit a rough patch in your relationships, commitment helps smooth the path again.

But **putting things right calls for 100 percent commitment**. It cannot be anything less. Commitment calls for tenacity, courage and a strong will from each of the persons involved. Falling in love, forming a friendship with someone, forming a team, is easy. But being committed to the relationship, even after the initial euphoria seems to fade, is tough. Keeping your relationship with your spouse, parents, siblings, friends or colleagues strong when misunderstandings and differences flare up could test the strength of your commitment to them.

That doesn't mean you have to compromise your own needs or bend over backward to fulfil unreasonable demands. That wouldn't be a sensible solution. It would only lead to bitterness and dissatisfaction in the long run. In personal relationships, if you truly care about the other person and your relationship with them, commitment is the lifeline that could help you hang in there, especially through difficult times. So, what does being committed mean?

Commitment means fully investing in supporting each other and the relationship, come what may. However, people sometimes move away from being committed. That could be to a personal relationship or a business project or some cause. The reasons are usually a natural inability to stay committed, lack of faith in the relationship or unwillingness to put in the effort or the time required to keep the commitment going. If you find you're wavering in your commitment, ask yourself why you want to opt out and then try and address that issue frankly with the other people in the relationship.

The power of commitment:

1. Commitment helps create stability and consistency

By making a commitment, we are promising ourselves that we have the commitment to follow through on what we say. As a result, we can feel stable and consistent in our own lives, which is critical for trust and relationship maintenance.

Think about a friendship that has been broken. Assume you followed through on your commitment and talked it through with your friend. There might have been a chance for the friendship to last if commitment had been shown. Possibilities arise from commitment.

2. Commitment is the key to success

Making disciplined and productive decisions is easier when you're willing to stretch yourself and live outside your comfort zone. There is no easy path to success, but commitment brings opportunities.

3. Integrity is bred by commitment

Integrity means staying true to our values and beliefs. Commitments are reflected in our actions. Stay focused on your goals because nothing comes easy in life. Those who believe in a better future for themselves and their families, will do whatever it takes to stay committed to them.

Here are a few tips for staying committed to a goal:

» Take time to consider your values and how achieving this commitment aligns with them.
» Keep yourself motivated and committed by visualising your goal being achieved.
» Review your plan on a regular basis, measure your progress and adapt it as needed.

TRUE HAPPINESS

True happiness comes from healing inner wounds by rewriting history and discovering your purpose.

My stint at the shelter was short but the experience brought about a pivotal shift in my thinking. I realised that life is much, much more than mere physical possessions or physical gratification. That true happiness comes from living a meaningful, useful life.

As it turned out, I got the wake-up call I badly needed at Hanover House. I needed to be reminded of what it was like to not have a house, to not have a comfortable life. The experience set me wondering about who had benefited more from the brief time I spent volunteering there: the traumatised women I'd inspired to believe that adversities could be overcome or me?

I wasn't a trained teacher or psychotherapist. Yet I'd succeeded in convincing those women that all wasn't lost and that they could trust me to help them. It taught me to appreciate what I had and discover the joy of leading a grateful life. In addition, it planted in my heart the seed of wanting to motivate people to take control of their lives.

A simpler truth my Hanover experience reminded me of is when we do good to others, we are actually doing ourselves a favour too. True and lasting happiness springs from a generous, compassionate heart, not from the things we own or from satisfying our own needs.

Just try it out. Try reaching out to someone in need, and you'll discover the immense joy that comes from knowing someone has overcome a problem or is breathing much easier or will be able to lead a better life because of the help you extended to them. You'll **discover the transformative power of true happiness.**

How to find your happy place and purpose:

1. Follow your heart instead of what others tell you to do

In the pursuit of personal happiness and healthy boundaries, cultivating self-awareness is vital. Achieving this depth of self-understanding isn't a simple task of merely digging deep; it involves acknowledging and healing inner wounds rooted in generational trauma or life experiences. Even those from supportive backgrounds may bear scars from life's imperfections. The key is tuning into oneself, exploring undiscovered aspects with the guidance of a mental health practitioner. Addressing hidden layers provides insight and the courage to pursue desires.

Once you identify your aspirations, the effort to turn dreams into reality becomes essential. Consider a person stuck in a bartending job, realising the lack of consistency and security. Through dedicated study, he earns an IT certification, securing a new job with a beginner's wage of $70,000 per year. It may seem modest, but it marks the beginning of stability, fulfilling subconscious cravings for security and stability. Understanding oneself leads to decisions aligned with genuine needs, paving the way for the true happiness sought. Don't shy away from taking risks or asserting your needs, even if they differ from others' expectations.

2. A constant need for validation will negatively affect your happiness

Often, our craving for approval and validation is rooted in the desire for feedback on our careers or accomplishments. When we share something, we subconsciously anticipate a response, viewing it as validation – why else would we bring it up?

Consider Nancy's story for a clearer understanding. Her father, preoccupied with work to make ends meet, unintentionally overlooked giving her the affirmation she deeply needed, especially from the man she loved most. Consequently, Nancy sought validation from others, believing it was about receiving feedback and growing. In reality, this stemmed from her unmet need for validation from her father. Everyone has unique stories shaping their unmet desires and needs.

While not a psychologist, I've personally grappled with deep trauma, spending much of my life in search of validation. As a speaker, I felt compelled to share everything, but after therapy and experiencing exhaustion from constant sharing, I reached a point where the need for validation diminished. I grew tired of sharing and yearned for privacy.

So, how can you stop seeking validation? It requires taking a pause and reflecting on why you're sharing. What is the purpose, the outcome and how will it enhance your life? Be brutally honest with yourself. Another crucial step is doing the internal work, seeking support from a trained therapist to gradually heal any wounds you may carry. This healing journey leads to a destination called 'PEACE,' and over time, this inner peace will make you question your need for external validation.

EXCELLENCE

Perfectionists tend to believe that if they're not perfect, they're a failure. Some demand perfectionism, not just from themselves, but from others as well. The others might be their spouse, children, parents, friends or work colleagues. No matter who they interact with, anything short of perfect is unacceptable to them. Perfection is an idealistic concept that advocates unrealistic expectations. And therefore, those who are fixated on it are more likely to be frustrated and unhappy in their life.

If you're one of those people who feel the compulsive need to be perfect or expect everything in your life to be perfect, you'd do well to acquaint yourself with the dangers of perfectionism. Striving for perfection, or even looking for it in others, could lead to dejection and stress and ultimately have an adverse effect on your health. When others can't meet your own idealistically high standards, that could also result in a lack of respect for them and erode your relationship. Perfectionists cannot accept mistakes, becoming rigid and excessively critical in their thinking and also developing unpleasant, disagreeable personalities.

That doesn't mean you should be satisfied with mediocrity. Rather, you should adopt a healthier approach toward expecting high standards. You should **look for excellence, not perfection.** Though both these are related to high standards, perfection implies impossibly high standards, whereas excellence results from a constant and healthy striving for improvement.

All human relationships need to be nurtured to keep them

healthy. But we need to nurture them to excellence, not strive to make them perfect. For example, if you're unhappy that you don't have a perfect spouse, you're forgetting that both of you are married to imperfect humans. By our very nature, we are all flawed. So, expecting perfection in a partner would be not only unfair but also unreasonable. There is room for improvement in almost all relationships, but by trying to achieve perfection, you would be setting yourself an impossible task. The sooner we accept the reality of human relationships, understand that they will be difficult and go through high and low points, the sooner we'll have a more balanced view of our own relationships.

A relationship that's excellent may not be perfect, but it's already way above the ordinary because the persons concerned constantly put in effort to improve it and make things better.

Achieving perfection can be unattainable and unrealistic, whereas striving for excellence can be more attainable and realistic. Here is a tip you can try:

» **Embracing Failure for Success**

Failure often serves as the stepping stone to success, providing valuable lessons that propel personal and professional growth. Consider my experience around Christmas in 2023 when I spoke for Dell in London, an event that led to overspending and a significant dent in my wallet. Surprisingly, this apparent failure became a catalyst for positive change in my spending habits. Instead of viewing it as a major setback, I reframed it, recognising it as the best spending decision that instilled lasting financial mindfulness.

In this transformative journey, the concept of neuroplasticity played a pivotal role. By consciously reframing my perspective on the failure, I engaged in the rewiring of my brain. This process involved forming new neural connections, cultivating a more mindful approach to financial decisions.

On a piece of paper, write the following:

1. Identify the Failure:

Clearly define the specific failure you experienced.

2. Analyse Three Key Points:

Break down the failure into three key points from your perspective.

3. Reframe the Experience

Under each point, reframe the failure by highlighting lessons learned and strategies to avoid repeating the mistake.

4. Engage in Writing

Actively write down your reflections, reinforcing the rewiring process in your subconscious.

UTILISE NEUROPLASTICITY

Understand that this practice aligns with neuroplasticity, allowing your brain to adapt and form new patterns through intentional mental exercises.

By incorporating these simple steps, you can turn failures into stepping stones for success. Writing down your reflections not only solidifies the learning process but actively engages neuroplasticity, ensuring lasting positive changes in your habits and thought patterns. Embrace failures as opportunities for growth, leveraging your brain's incredible capacity to adapt and form new pathways toward success. **Don't let failure get you down.** Instead, embrace it as a learning experience. You can learn and grow from failures because they are inevitable parts of the learning process. Excellence is achieved through learning from our failures. Practice self-compassion. Be kind and understanding towards yourself when you make mistakes or fall short of your goals.

SELF-CONFIDENCE

If you want to achieve your heart's desires and succeed in life, then self-confidence won't be something optional. It will be a must. Those who aren't self-confident can never reach their goals. And neither can they stand up for themselves, act on their desires, start a new venture or take on bigger responsibilities. Sadly, those who don't do anything about their lack of self-confidence will find it next to impossible to live life to the fullest.

Self-confidence is a strong belief in our abilities, self-worth, and judgement. It fills us with the courage to make difficult decisions and take control of our lives. It's one of the first qualities we need to succeed. In fact, **self-confidence sets the foundation for success**.

But what if you're basically shy by nature? Or timid? Is it possible for you to develop confidence in yourself? Of course it is. Even the most fainthearted can transform themselves into bold and self-confident individuals. One way to begin is by setting small achievable goals for yourself. With every minor goal you achieve, you'll grow in self-confidence and be ready to attempt larger ones. Like in my case. Speaking in front of smaller groups of people gave me the confidence to address and motivate much larger ones.

Another way is to train your mind to believe in yourself and to accept that you need to change your behaviour and body language to simulate that of self-confident people. This will help you develop, not only a more attractive personality, but also your inherent talents and skills. Rewiring your brain so you can think positively and make meaningful life changes is possible because of something called neuroplasticity. This is the ability of the brain to change its structure and function in response to different experiences.

Earlier, neuroscientists believed the brain was mouldable or plastic only in the first few years of our life. But modern research has shown that our brain is constantly growing new neurons and changing its networks and circuits throughout our life. The more often we repeat a thought or emotion or action, the stronger the related brain connections become. That explains why the more often we practise doing something, the better we get at it. Also, each time we learn something new, we're creating new pathways and connections between our brain cells.

So yes, our brain can be rewired to enhance our confidence levels. Daily exercise, positive self-talk, meditation, and visualisation are some of the ways this can be done. For instance, if you regularly make time each day to visualise a goal you lack the confidence to pursue, this vision will be firmly fixed in your brain. Then, when you actually start working toward achieving it, instead of self-doubts and negative thoughts, what you envision will dominate your mind and you'll find the confidence in yourself to make it a reality. Just a small example. But I guess you get the picture.

INNER PEACE

To dwell in my own cocoon is to embrace tranquillity.

Our world today seems full of conflict and pain, one nation up in arms against another, one community rising against another. And as if that wasn't enough, we are still feeling the impact of the way the COVID-19 pandemic raged across the world and claimed millions of lives. The world's population is more in need of inner peace now than ever before.

However, inner peace isn't controlled by external conditions or factors like your financial status, your educational background, or which part of the world you live in. It is related to emotional well-being and how strong you are mentally. It implies a sense of internal harmony, knowledge of self, and feeling fulfilled in life.

A state of inner peace frees your mind of negative thoughts, anxieties and fears. It unblocks your creative energy, keeps you calm as you handle the daily activities of your life and improves your relationships with others. **Inner peace helps you see things in a new light.**

To have a peaceful mind, you don't have to retire to the Himalayas or some remote island or a quiet place free of chaos. Inner peace is a skill that can be learned and experienced wherever you are.

So how can we enjoy inner peace? Let's see some of the major techniques we could practise.

Acceptance: This brings me full circle, back to the first life lesson: accepting the things we cannot change. The moment you accept that you cannot change any negative experiences you had in the past, those experiences begin to lose their power over your mind and, ultimately, you'll be able to let go of them and turn to things you can control. It could even be a situation you find yourself in today. Say you find yourself stuck in traffic just when you're on your way to an important meeting. Instead of fretting and fuming over the state of affairs, practice accepting the way things are, having patience and going with the flow.

Self-acceptance: This, in a way, is related to the first step. It means a complete acceptance of yourself as you are, the way you look, what you have, who you are, faults, deficiencies, past mistakes, and all. Self-acceptance calms your inner critic, makes you stop blaming yourself for everything that's gone wrong in your life and lets you embrace yourself, love yourself. Self-love, in turn, leads to self-improvement and a more balanced outlook on life.

An attitude of gratefulness: Instead of being hurt and resentful about the things you don't have, try and focus on whatever is good in your life, however minor, the things you should be grateful for. In other words, count your blessings. This exercise will instantly lift your mood. Regularly practising techniques like these will help you make steady progress on the road to finding inner peace.

Experience inner peace in your own life:

1. Experience calmness in nature

Being in nature and experiencing inner peace are closely related concepts. In terms of mind and body, nature has a powerful, calming effect. Natural surroundings can reduce stress, anxiety and increase feelings of well-being and inner peace.

By providing a sense of calm and tranquillity, nature can have a therapeutic effect on the mind, helping to reduce stress and anxiety. In addition to helping us to focus on the present, being surrounded by natural beauty can also help us to let go of our concerns and worries.

2. Spirituality and letting go

As a metaphor, 'letting go and letting God' describes surrendering control to a higher power. During difficult times, it can provide a sense of calm and inner peace. Trust in the belief that things will work out for the best, even if you don't understand how or why. Keep in mind that 'letting go and letting God' looks different for each person, depending on your own spiritual connections, or lack of them, and finding your own approach that is meaningful to you may take time and practice.

3. Pets bring inner peace

My therapist told me to get a dog, to help me heal from the ravages of PTSD. Today, I have a Moodle and a Cavoodle. (Aki and KoKo)

Animal-assisted therapy, also known as pet therapy, can contribute to inner peace. It has been found that animals, especially pets, have a calming and soothing effect on people. It is believed that pets can help reduce stress and anxiety and increase feelings of inner peace by providing a sense of comfort and companionship. In addition to providing non-judgmental, unconditional love, pets have been shown to improve self-esteem and self-worth and can also help improve mental health conditions such as depression, anxiety and PTSD.

A PURPOSE IN LIFE

A prerequisite for grasping what you want to be is discovering your purpose in life. Ultimately, **having a purpose in life makes life worth living**. It doesn't matter if it's just an immediate desire to create a better life for you and your family, like it was for me when I had to fend for my son and myself, or a long-term objective of establishing a successful business, or anything else. The journey of resolutely making your dream a reality will not only give you opportunities to think creatively but also help keep negative thoughts at bay. At every step you'll be reminded you have something to achieve, something to live for.

I learned first-hand what a difference having a purpose in life can make. It can even drive you to achieve the impossible, like holding an international event like I did without any prior experience of organising a mega-contest like that.

Even in the time of the COVID-19 pandemic and the lockdowns that kept people confined to their homes and made businesses grind to a halt, I decided to make meaningful use of my time at home. I set newer goals for myself. Despite having no professional work at hand, I kept busy. I didn't stay home and ponder over the negative impacts of the pandemic. Instead, I focused on thinking of ways to make life better, not for me but for the underprivileged. I got involved in philanthropic efforts in South Africa. I did online keynote presentations. I studied. I grew a veggie patch, made candlelit dinners for my children almost every night. My goal was to be busy, do good and look at everything in the most positive light. Negativity has no place in my home, let alone in my mind.

These are the choices I've made. What you choose to make your purpose in life could be far different. Choices are plentiful. But how well we choose and how effectively we strategise things... that's entirely up to us.

How to identify your purpose – and live it:

1. Connect the dots

Connect the dots between your past and your present. Your purpose will be revealed along the way. At the tender age of 23, I was the organiser of Miss India International for Australia. I learned to understand my audience, and today, two decades later, I'm still working with an audience on stage. Perhaps this was always my destiny.

There are clues in your life. All you have to do is cultivate calm and peace to see them for what they are. What is your method for finding clues? You will hear the roar of the signs in the silence.

2. Your passion drives your purpose

Knowing your purpose will give you joy and meaning.

What's the point of spending your entire life working at a job that makes you unhappy? If you are unhappy in your position at a corporate firm, consider changing roles within the company to find a role that aligns with your passion. It is what you bring to yourself that brings you joy.

3. Make the most of your life

The future is not guaranteed for anyone, so live life as though each day is your last. The more you live life to the fullest, the more opportunities and possibilities you will have around you. The glass is half-empty when you see it half-empty. Identifying your purpose and living a joyful life are possible with conviction if you see the glass as half-full.

As we reach the conclusion of my story, I hope this book has been a source of inspiration and practical guidance. I firmly believe that no obstacle we encounter is insurmountable. Life is a fleeting flame—bright and vibrant, yet all too brief.

www.ingramcontent.com/pod-product-compliance
Lightning Source LLC
Chambersburg PA
CBHW011232160426
43209CB00010B/1563